Young Chef Cookbook

The Complete Baking Book for Kids Who Love to Bake and Eat

Funny and Healthy Recipes to Prepare with Parents and Share with Friends (Baking Class for Every Age)

Junior Health Institute

Table of Contents

Introduction

Congratulations on purchasing **Kid Chef: Young Chef Cookbook - The Complete Baking Book for Kids Who Love to Bake and Eat** and thank you for doing so!

The following chapters will discuss everything you need to know about cooking so you can make delicious meals for your friends and family. These recipes are sure to impress and satisfy anyone who comes to your table. In these chapters, you will find all the information you will need to go from a beginner's understanding of baking and how it works to an intermediate level that will allow you to prepare a large meal for everyone you love to enjoy! Whether you're looking to learn how to bake muffins for a friend or make a flatbread pizza, this book can help you to get the information you need. The information in this book will fill you with confidence and allow you to try all sorts of new and delicious things. If you're looking for some good reasons to learn how to bake, here some great ones!

Baking is a great creative outlet and a great way to let off steam.

If you're learning how to bake, you will find that working with the dough and pounding it out is a great way to let off the steam of a long school day or a long week. Stressed out thinking about report cards or that exam? Try beating up some pizza dough until you can make something amazingly delicious out of it!

Learning how to bake expands your mind and helps you to understand more about flavors and customs of the world around you.

Baking new and wonderful things from all around the world can show you a lot about the flavors and customs that come from all over the world. Learning about new cultures and their customs helps us to be more connected as a human race, and allows us to be more open to other new experiences in the future.

Baking your own delicious items can save you lots of money while keeping your home stocked with some of the most delicious foods that you'll love to have time and time again!

Buying brownies, for instance, at the bakery can cost as much as $15 for a nice, big batch! When you make your own brownies at home, whether from a mix or from scratch, you will be saving an average of about a dollar per brownie! With savings like that, it's a wonder anyone ever lets professionals do their baking for them, right? Well, if you get nice and experienced at making baked goods on your own, you can be the person that all your friends and family call when they're looking for the most delicious baked goods that anyone can make!

You can also bake for yourself and keep your favorite delicious treats on hand whenever you want them. Could you imagine having homemade chocolate chip cookies in the kitchen all the time because you made a batch, and they're still around for you to snack on? Jackpot!

You can share your favorite things with the people around you, and baking with people you care about is always a wonderful bonding experience.

Baking with the people that we know and love can be such a wonderful bonding experience. Learning together, rolling up your sleeves, talking about the recipe, getting to know more about how baking works and how each of the ingredients interact with one another and working together to make something truly delicious is a wonderful way to spend time with someone that you care about. Consider finding a recipe that you and friends can follow the next time they come over to visit, once you've gained a little bit of baking skill of your own. Consider having an adult help you to roll out your own dough to make biscuits or croissants for the morning after an awesome sleepover with your pals!

Expressing yourself through baking is a wonderful way to go.

When you start to learn more about baking, and you start to remember how to make certain things on your own, you will find that you can express yourself and make your own wonderful creations in the kitchen. What an excellent feeling!

GLOSSARY

A

Acidulate (Verb) – To add acid to something to brighten the flavors or to cut through the fatty properties of a dish.

Al Dente (Adjective) – When food (typically pasta) still has a slight firmness to it when bitten. This is achieved by cooking your pasta for slightly less time than usual.

B

Bake (Verb) – To use an oven or enclosed and indirect heat source for cooking foods.

Barbecue (Verb) – To cook foods, typically meat over an open flame. This is usually done outdoors and can incorporate other elements like wood smoking.

Baste (Verb) – To shower a meat with either melted butter or its own juices periodically throughout cooking to ensure the meat stays moist over the heat.

Batter (Noun) – A mixture of flour and liquid that forms a coating for foods, which will then crisp when being deep-fried.

Batter (Verb) – To coat a piece of food in a mixture of flour and liquid before deep-frying.

Beat (Verb) – To use a whisk, fork, or mixer to work air into a mixture and to get the mixture evenly-colored.

Blanch (Verb) – To briefly scald a fruit or vegetable in boiling water, then remove it and plunge into an ice bath to immediately stop the cooking process.

Blend (Verb) – To thoroughly mix all ingredients together with the help of a blade to get things into a uniform, liquid texture.

Blind Bake (Noun) – The process of baking something, usually a pie crust, before the rest of its components to ensure all elements are done cooking at the same time.

Boil (Verb) – To heat water to 212° Fahrenheit or 100° Celcius, at which point bubbles form in the water, and it begins to turn to vapor.

Boil (Verb) – To cook food in boiling water.

Bone (Verb) – To remove all the bones from a piece of meat before cooking, typically done with a whole fish or chicken to make consumption easier.

Braise (Verb) – To lightly fry food and then strew it slowly in a closed pot or container.

Bread (Verb) – To coat food in breadcrumbs before cooking, to give it a crunchy, bready coating.

Broil (Verb) – To cook meat or fish in indirect heat, as in an oven, at a very high temperature so as to cook the food faster, and typically the food should be turned at least once during cooking.

Brown (Verb) – To cook meat (typically used in reference to ground meat) to change its pale or pink color to brown, indicating that it has been heated through and is now safe to eat.

C

Caramelize (Verb) – To heat food during cooking, so it creates a pleasant, crisp, brown coating on the sides that touched the pan.

Chop (Verb) – To cut food into roughly bite-sized pieces using quick, heavy strokes with your knife. These cuts are typically somewhat inconsistent and less measured than others. If a recipe calls for items to be "finely chopped," it means that the pieces should be about half of bite-size. If a recipe calls for items to be "roughly chopped," it means the pieces should be slightly larger than bite-sized.

Clarify (Verb) – Typically with butter, to heat and remove impurities from a liquid by skimming them off the top or straining them. This can also be done when making your own broth or stock.

Core (Verb) – To remove the center section or core of a fruit. With an apple, this can be done with a vegetable peeler, an apple core, or it can be done with a knife if the person is highly skilled.

Cream (Verb) – The technique or softening a solid fat like butter or lard into a smooth mass, then blending it in with the other ingredients. This is most common in baking and can be done to make a smooth buttercream icing or a cookie dough.

Crumb (noun) – The pattern and size of the holes that form inside a cake or loaf that has been baked. For example, breads that are made with high-moisture dough are typically said to have an open and irregular crumb. Close-textured crumb comes for a drier dough.

Cube (Verb) – To cut into cubes. Typically your recipe will tell you how large the cubes should be, but one-inch cubes are typical.

Cut In (Verb) – To distribute a solid fat into your flour by using cutting motions with 2 knives in a scissor-like motion or by using a pastry blender until evenly divided into very tiny pieces.

D

Dash (Noun) – In many recipes, you will hear them call for "a dash of" an ingredient. Typically, a dash is roughly 1/16th of a teaspoon or 4-5 drops of a liquid; it's a very small amount that is just enough to add a hint of that flavor.

Deep-Fry (Verb) – Also known as "Deep fat frying," is a cooking method that calls for foods to be submerged into very hot oil. The oil should typically be heated to 375°

Fahrenheit or 190° Celsius, but your recipe will often tell you if the oil will deviate from that. The fat used for this process can vary, but typical oils used are peanut oil, canola oil, vegetable oil, or lard.

Deglaze (Verb) – To heat a liquid, typically an acidic one like wine, to dissolve the browned, caramelized residue on the bottom of the pan to turn it into a sauce, soup, or gravy. This browned residue is known as "fond," which can also be found in this glossary.

Degrease (Verb) – To remove the fat or grease from the surface of a soup, sauce, stew, etc.with a spoon, bulb baster, strainer, or other helpful implement.

Deseed (Verb) – To take the seeds out of a fruit or vegetable.

Devein (Verb) – To remove the delicate black vein that runs along the back of a shrimp. Once the shell is removed or split along the back of the shrimp, this vein is revealed, and can simply be gently pried out with the tip of a paring knife and loosely pulled.

9

Dice (Verb) – To cut food into small cubes for even cooking. When dicing vegetables, it is important to dice all the pieces into a similar size. Your recipe will sometimes tell you how big your dices should be, but about ¾ of an inch is typical for the size of a dice.

Dilute (Verb) – To thin a liquid or mixture by adding more liquid to it, or to reduce the intensity of a flavor by adding liquid to it.

Dissolve (Verb) – To combine one ingredient with another to form a solution, as you would when you dissolve sugar in water.

Dissolve (Verb) – To melt or liquefy an ingredient, as you would with either butter or chocolate.

Dollop (Noun) – A generous spoonful of a creamy or cohesive mixture that has been removed from the spoon with one firm flick of the wrist. One can also create the trademark round shape of a dollop by forming the mixture or cream.

Dot (Verb) – To place small bits or pieces of ingredients over, within, or around another ingredient, so as to achieve an even distribution of the first ingredient. For instance, you can dot pizza dough with cheese to ensure that the cheese melts evenly over the surface of the pie.

Dredge (Verb) – To coat wet or moistened foods with a dry ingredient prior to cooking. For instance, a piece of chicken that has been marinating in buttermilk can be dredged through a mixture of flour, herbs, and spices before being made into fried chicken.

Dress (Verb) – To prepare food for cooking or serving so that it's pleasing to the eye, as you would dress a roasted turkey on holiday.

Dress (Verb) – To coat with a dressing or mixture in order to change or enhance the flavor, as you would with a salad.

Drippings (Noun) – The juices and fat remaining in the pan after the meat has been cooked. Drippings are commonly used in making sauces and gravies.

Drizzle (Verb) – To pour a very fine stream of a liquid, condiment, or syrup over a food in a decorative or pleasing pattern. This scatters the flavor all over the food, while also looking pleasing to the eye.

Dry-Fry (Verb) – to cook foods that are high in fat in a non-stick pan with no additional fat than what naturally comes from the meat that is being cooked.

Dust (Verb) – To lightly sprinkle a fine layer of powdered or granulated ingredients over or onto good. You can dust your French toast with powdered sugar for a little extra sweetness.

E

Emulsify (Verb) – To mix something completely together, so it becomes an emulsion.

Emulsion (Noun) – A liquid that is made of two or more liquids and other ingredients that have been completely mixed together to create a liquid of a new texture, as one would with oil and vinegar dressing.

F

Fillet (Noun) – A boneless piece of meat, poultry, or fish that is one thickness the whole way through.

Fillet (Verb) – To cut a piece of meat, so it is one uniform thickness the whole way through.

Flake (Verb) – To pull apart the natural seams of a protein, typically fish, so it can be combined with other ingredients.

Flambé (Verb) – To cook with a sprinkling of alcohol that allows the pan to burst into flames for several seconds, to add crust and flavor to the food in the pan.

Flute (Verb) – To make a decorative edge or pattern in pastry before it is baked, leaving the final product with a very pleasing and decorative design.

Fold (Verb) – A very precise term used for both cooking and baking, which calls for the careful combining of two ingredients or mixtures which have two different thicknesses or weights. This is accomplished by placing one ingredient on top of your mixture, pushing a large mixing spoon down to the bottom of the mixture, and lifting up, tucking the new ingredient into the mixture, thus keeping its texture and density more or less intact.

Fond (Noun) – From the French word for "base," the browned, caramelized residue left on the bottom of the pan after cooking meat and or vegetables, which can be deglazed and used for causes, soups, gravies, etc.

Fricassee (Noun) – A cooking method that combines both wet and dry heat. Fricassee falls between a sauté, in which no liquid is added, and a stew, which does contain liquids. Chicken fricassee is a traditional French dish that has a creamy white sauce.

Fry (Verb) – To cook food in hot oil or fat, whether by plunging the food into the fat or by cooking in a shallower pan of fat to get the desired crisp texture.

G

Garnish (Noun) – A decoration used to make your dish look more pleasing to the eye. You may have seen baked fish served with slices of lemon, or a cooked piece of chicken served over a bed of green lettuce. These bits are not meant to be eaten but are simply meant to be pleasing to the eye.

Garnish (Verb) – To add a decoration or embellishment to the plate as a way to please the eye of your diners.

Glaze (Noun) – A glossy coating that one can put on food, typically by pouring, dipping, dipping, or drizzling. Many glazes have flavors, some sweet, and some savory. Some glazes, like egg whites, are simply there to aid in keeping food looking glossy after their time in the oven.

Grate (Verb) – To shred an ingredient by dragging it over a grater or a rough surface meant to shred or break up food. Cheese and carrots can often be grated. Hash browns, before they are cooked, are grated potatoes.

Gratin (Noun) – A culinary technique that dictates an ingredient is topped with a browned crust, often using breadcrumbs, grated cheese, egg, or butter. Baked macaroni and cheese with a breadcrumb topping is a popular example of this.

Grease (Verb) – To rub down a pan or cooking dish with an oily or greasy substance such as non-stick spray, shortening, lard, butter, or oil, so the food that's in it doesn't get stuck to it during the baking process.

Grill (Verb) – To cook over a dry heat, typically direct heat, as one would on a grill outside. Grilling can happen indoors on a grill pan, but one misses the flavors, and unique caramelization one can get from direct heat. Grilling is almost always accompanied by linear markings on either side of the food that was grilled.

Grind (Verb) – To use a tool to crush something into smaller, more easily usable, or digestible pieces. One should grind peppercorns to make pepper, as it makes it much easier to eat and digest.

J

Julienne (Noun) – A style of cutting vegetables that leaves the pieces in very thin square sticks.

K

Knead (Verb) – To mix a pliable dough by stretching, adding pressure, and rolling your palms into the dough. This forms gluten in the flour and makes it more pliable as you go.

Knock Back (Verb) – After a bread dough's first rise, to press it back down to burst the tiny air bubbles that have formed in the dough. This forces the bubbles to reform again in the shape and size that you want, which results in a smoother texture.

L

Lukewarm (Noun) – A temperature that is just slightly warmer than room temperature. It's not hot or particularly warm, but it's not cold, either.

m

Marinade (Noun) – A sauce that is usually made with things like spices, oil, vinegar, herbs, and items that will be used to soak raw meat before it is cooked and then eaten.

Marinate (Verb) – To allow a piece of meat or vegetables to sit in a flavorful sauce or liquid mixture to gain flavor for no less than 30 minutes, and up to 48 hours before cooking.

Mince (Verb) – To cut up or grind an ingredient into very small pieces. Typically, this word refers to meat, but it can be used for things such as garlic, which are meant to be used in very small pieces from time to time.

Mix (Verb) – To thoroughly combine ingredients together using a spoon to stir them all together.

P

Pan-broil (Verb) – To cook something, such as thin steaks fillets, or chops, in a pan on the stovetop, taking care to remove any fat that accumulates in the pan, such as with a turkey baster or a spoon.

Pan-fry (Verb) – To cook in a pan on the stovetop, using just enough fat or oil to keep the food from sticking and to form a tasty crust on either side of the food.

Pan-sear (Verb) – To cook in the pan at high temperature until a browned crust forms, before resuming cooking in another method such as baking, braising, grilling, sautéing, roasting, and more.

Parboil (Verb) – To cook food in boiling water until it's partially cooked. This is a way of cooking that uses no oil, which then allows you to add color and caramelization to the food for the remainder of the cooking process.

Pare (Verb) – To remove the skin of a fruit or vegetable using either a paring knife or vegetable peeler.

Peel (Verb) – To remove the skin of a fruit or vegetable using your hands, a paring knife, or a vegetable peeler as is needed.

Pickle (Verb) – To preserve by placing in a seasoned vinegar or brine mixture. Just about any food can be pickled!

Pinch (Noun) - In many recipes, you will hear them call for "a pinch of" an ingredient. Typically, a pinch is roughly $1/16^{th}$ of a teaspoon or 4-5 drops of a liquid; it's a very small amount that is just enough to add a hint of that flavor.

Pit (Noun) – The hard center of a fruit like a peach, which must be removed before complete consumption of the fruit.

Pit (Noun) – A method of barbecue that calls for burying encased meat and vegetables under the surface of the earth and a source of heat.

Plank Cooking (Noun) – A method of cooking that calls for a plank of seasoned flavorful wood (such as hickory) to be cooked underneath meat so that the meat can take on the flavors while being cooked in the oven by either baking or broiling.

Plump (Verb) – To rehydrate or to restore moisture to a food item that has been dehydrated.

Poach (Verb) – To submerge a food under a liquid, such as stock, broth, milk, or water for long enough to cook it. This is considered different from boiling or other wet methods of heating, as the temperature of the liquid is kept relatively low at about 160°-180° Fahrenheit, or 71°-82° Celsius.

Purée (Noun) – A smooth mixture of cooked food that has been blended, ground, pressed, or strained to be the consistency of a creamy paste.

Purée (Verb) – Blend, grind, press, or strain cooked food, so it takes on the consistency of a creamy paste.

Help monsters find their food

R

Reduce (Verb) – To thicken a sauce or liquid mixture by simmering overheat until much of the liquid content evaporates.

Reduction (Noun) – A sauce that has been made using the process of reducing.

Refresh (Verb) – To submerge cooked food. Usually, this is done with vegetables, into an ice bath or under cold running water, to stop further cooking and to retain its vibrant color.

Render (Verb) – To slowly cook the fat out of a meat over low heat, and over a long period of time, so the fat becomes a liquid, rather than crisping up on the bottom of the pan. The fat that has been rendered can be used for other dishes.

Roast (Verb) – To cook using dry heat with no covering in temperatures starting at, at least or 300° Fahrenheit 150° Celsius. Cooking the food in an oven with no covering allows you to get a crispy layer on the outside of your dish, whereas coverings such as foil tend to keep moisture closed in on your dish.

S

Sauté (Verb) – To cook food quickly in a minimal amount of oil or fat over higher heat.

Scald (Verb) – To heat milk over an indirect source and to heat the milk until just before it's boiling. When small bubbles form around the edges, you have reached the scalding point of milk.

Scallop (Verb) – To cook in Gratin style.

Score (Verb) – To make shallow cuts on the surface of your meat, fish, cakes, bread, etc.that can be decorative or which can aid in the cooking and absorption of flavor.

Sear (Verb) – To cook in the pan at high temperature until a browned crust forms, before resuming cooking in another method such as baking, braising, grilling, sautéing, roasting, and more.

Season (Verb) – To add herbs, seasonings, juices, condiments, and spices to enhance and change its flavor or taste.

Shallow Fry (Verb) – To cook portion-sized cuts of food in a pan filled with one to two inches of oil. Foods are partially submitted into the hot oil and flipped halfway through to promote even cooking.

Shred (Verb) – To shred an ingredient by dragging it over a grater or a rough surface meant to shred or break up food. Or to use forks to pull apart cooked meat such as pork or chicken, so it's somewhat fibrous. Cheese and carrots can often be shredded. Hash browns, before they are cooked, are grated potatoes.

Shuck (Verb) – To remove the shell or outer casing of seafood or vegetables.

Sift (Verb) – To shake or grind a powder through a sieve or a strainer, so the powder has no lumps or large pieces in it.

Simmer (Verb) – To keep food on the heat, just below the boiling point to help flavors to develop and sauces to thicken.

Skim (Verb) – To use a spoon or other tool to pull congealed fat from the top of a soup, sauce or stew, or to remove impurities from a broth or stock as they're being pulled from the bones.

Slice (Verb) – To use a sharp knife to make thin, precise cuts, as one would do with a cucumber.

Smidgen (Noun) – In many recipes, you will hear them call for "a smidgen of" an ingredient. Typically, a pinch is roughly 1/16th of a teaspoon or 4-5 drops of a liquid; it's a very small amount that is just enough to add a hint of that flavor.

Steam (Verb) – To expose food to hot steam, which brings the food to full cooked temperature. This can be done by placing a metal grate over boiling water and placing the food on the grate.

Steep (Verb) – To submerge dry ingredients like spices, herbs, coffee, and tea in hot water, and to leave them to soak for long enough for the flavors to extract from those ingredients.

Stew (Noun) – A thick, hearty soup that has been cooked for a long period of time over a low heat to develop flavors, and to reduce the moisture in the mixture.

Stew (Verb) – To slowly cook a mixture of liquid and solid ingredients over low heat for flavors to develop and for the liquid to thicken.

Stir (Verb) – To thoroughly combine ingredients together using a spoon to mix them all together.

Stir-Fry (Noun) – A dish which is made of roughly chopped vegetables, meat, and soy sauce, which is lightly oiled and cooked all at once in a large pan such as a wok. Typically served over rice.

Stir-Fry (Verb) – To cook food in such a manner.

T

Toss (Verb) – To shake a bowl or pan, which contains both food and sauce, so as to thoroughly coat the food in the sauce.

W

Whip (Verb) – To vigorously mix an ingredient in such a way that incorporates air throughout it. Egg whites and heavy cream can be whipped into a much lighter, fluffier texture.

Whisk (Noun) – A cooking utensil which has a network of stiff wires that allow air to be whipped into ingredients and to thoroughly mix things such as eggs into a cohesive texture.

Z

Zest (Noun) – The shredded rind of a citrus fruit.

Zest (Verb) – To shred the rind off of a citrus fruit.

CHAPTER 1: NUTRITIONAL VALUES EXPLAINED

This chapter will cover something that you have no doubt seen on the packaging of some of your favorite foods! These are called Nutritional Facts labels, and they give you the total picture of all the different things that are in your foods, so you know if and when you're eating too much or just enough!

Nutrition Facts

8 servings per container

Serving size	2/3 cup (55g)

Amount per serving

Calories 230

% Daily Value *

Total Fat 8g	10%
Saturated Fat 1g	5%
Trans Fat 0g	
Cholesterol 0mg	0%
Sodium 160mg	7%
Total Carbohydrate 37g	13%
Dietary Fiber 4g	14%
Total Sugars 12g	
Protein 3g	
Vitamin D 2mcg	10%
Calcium 260mg	20%
Iron 8mg	45%
Potassium 235mg	6%

You want to make sure that your daily intake (how much you're eating) of each thing isn't too much and that you're getting all the right vitamins, fats, minerals, calories, proteins, and more. These labels help you to know all about what's really in your food, and how much you should be eating. For instance, did you know that some of your favorite crunchy, cheesy snacks are only supposed to be eaten by about a handful at a time? These labels tell you all kinds of things about the foods you're eating.

The facts on these labels often cover:
- How many servings are in the whole container (box, bag, etc.) (A serving is how much of something you should be eating in one sitting)
- How big a serving size is in cups, ounces, grams, etc.
- How many calories are in each serving
- How much of each nutrient such as protein and fat are in each serving
- How many vitamins and minerals are in each serving
- The percentage of your daily values that each of those numbers represents.

Daily values are how much of each nutrient you're supposed to get in each day. So, if this label says that 8g of fat is 10% of your daily value, you can do a little bit of math to find that the total daily recommended value of fat is ten times that, or 80g. By looking at these nutritional facts labels, we can know more about what's in the foods we're eating and it can help us to make sure that our bodies are getting all the things they should be getting, while not getting too much of the things that we should only have in small amounts.

Sodium is one of the things that you will want to monitor as you get older. Eating too much sodium from day to day can cause some problems in your body and can cause your health to drop in ways that aren't too pleasant. You don't want to feel less than your best because you're not eating all the right things, right? These labels can help us to stay within the recommended daily limits of these things, so we stay nice and healthy. Thanks to these labels, we can know all the things that are in the foods we're eating, we can make sure tha we're not having too many of the bad things, we can have more of the good things, and we can feel great while we're doing it.

One of the things you've probably heard people talking about watching their carbohydrate intake. Carbohydrates come from starchy or sugary foods like potatoes and fruit, as well as things like chips and candy. Some people like to limit their carbohydrates to about 200 grams each day, while people who are very active and who have careers in sports or fitness will tend to have lots more because they need the energy.

Calories is one of the things that people will tend to count the most, which is why it's one of the biggest numbers on the Nutritional Facts label. It's recommended that people who are trying to maintain their weight (which means that they're not trying to lose or gain weight) take in about 2,000 calories each day. Doing this gives you enough energy to get through your day without getting groggy and tired, but doesn't give you so many calories that you start to put on weight. Your doctor can tell you just how many calories you should be eating each day in order to keep yourself feeling healthy and strong.

Let's do a little experiment involving the Nutritional Facts labels in your house! Go into your kitchen and see how many Nutritional Facts labels you can find in just five minutes. As you find them, take a look at them and see what's in each thing. Are any of the higher or lower in calories, fat, protein, and carbohydrates than you expected them to be? Take your notes here below!

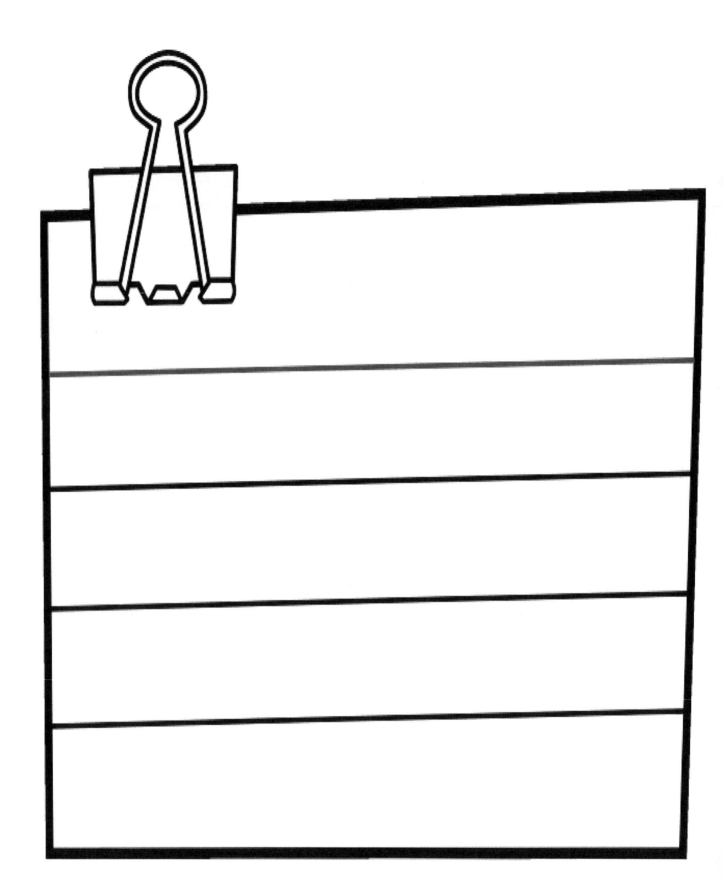

Chapter 2: Most Common Ingredients

As you get more and more comfortable with baking, you will realize more of the things that you like to use and the things that you need more than others. Each of the items in this chapter are not created equal, and some of them you may never need at all, but these are some kitchen basics that you should get familiar with if you're going to be baking or cooking more regularly.

Oils and Fats

Butter – Butter is a classic fat for cooking and for baking that has many, many purposes and a delicious flavor. Some people prefer to cut out butter, as it's high in fat and it might not be the healthiest fat to use when cooking. When it comes to baking, there are few substitutes that are as effective and delicious.

Olive Oil – Olive oil is a wonderful fat for multipurpose use and cooking. There are some breads (like focaccia) that require the hefty use of olive oil, and it's a great staple to have on hand.

Shortening – Shortening is used most commonly in baking and is a great fat to use for things like flaky biscuits, but you may or may not find that it works best for you. It's fairly inexpensive, and it lasts for a long time. There are even vegetable substitutes on the market if you're looking for something healthier.

Vegetable Oil – This is your essential, all-purpose oil. It's great for lubricating pans, frying, baking, and for recipes that call for a lot of oil because it's inexpensive and comes readily in large quantities. Canola oil is another oil that falls into this category, and it comes down to a matter of preference.

Vinegars

Balsamic Vinegar – This is a dark and robust vinegar that is good for salad dressings, sauces for chicken, and more. You might not find a lot of use for this in baking, but in recipes that call for it, it's hard to substitute it.

Red Wine Vinegar – This is a lighter vinegar that goes along well with flavors like Dijon and can be used in sauces and dressings. Neither of these vinegars can easily be substituted for the other.

Baking

Baking Powder – This is the founder of the white baking generations, and it is actually a mixture of baking soda, cream of tartar, and sometimes cornstarch. Be sure, when looking at your recipes, that you do not get this mixture confused with baking soda.

Baking Soda – Also known as bicarbonate of soda or sodium bicarbonate is the coarser of the white baking generations. This is usually used with a ratio of about ¼ tsp. to every cup of flour.

Brown Sugar – Brown sugar is stickier than white or granulated sugar, making it great for binding cookies. If you're looking to make softer, chewy cookies, brown sugar is something you'll want to have on hand!

Cake Flour – The protein content (gluten) in cake flour is slightly lower than all-purpose flour, resulting in a better texture for your cakes. If you like to make cakes and cupcakes from scratch, this is the flour you'll want to use!

Chocolate Chips – Having chocolate chips on hand at all times can be difficult if you're prone to snacking, but it's always good to have some on hand if you suddenly need to make some chocolate chip cookies, bread, or pancakes.

Cocoa Powder – This dark powder might not taste very good on its own (trust me, it doesn't), but with cocoa powder, sugar, and some other ingredients, brownies are just a few minutes away!

Corn Starch – This is mostly used for thickening, but it's a great product to have in your cabinet. It lasts for a long time, you don't need very much for each use, and it does its job very well.

Flour – You can use flour to make a wide variety of things from pancakes to batters and doughs, and you would do well to keep some on hand at all times. You just never know when you're going to need flour for a recipe, whether you're big into baking or not.

Powdered Sugar – Powdered sugar is one of those things that can't be substituted for another kind of sugar, no matter which way you slice it. If you have some powdered sugar on hand, you can always whip up some nice icing with nothing more than a little bit of milk and vanilla extract.

Sprinkles – Just like everything else in this baker's list, these can come in handy when you least expect it.

Sugar – Sugar can be used to even out the acidity or saltiness of a sauce or a dish and can be used in large part for baking as well. There are a lot of reasons one might need sugar, including for coffee and tea, so it's great to have on hand.

Vanilla Extract – Vanilla extract can be used for baking, but it can also be used to make complex and delicious flavors in other dishes that aren't even sweet! There are no limits to the amazing things you can do in the kitchen.

Yeast – Yeast will make your bread rise, and you will likely need it unless you have self-rising flour. Yeast is a classic way to go, and it's inexpensive.

Seasonings

Chili Powder – This is actually a compound mixture that contains a lot of various things. Using chili powder, you can make things like your own chili, your own nachos, your own tacos, and some pretty delicious soups and stews.

Cinnamon – This is a classic that can be used on just about anything from your morning oatmeal to some delicious muffins. You can even use the cinnamon to help develop savory flavors and to give them just a hint of spice without the heat.

Cumin – If you've had Latin food and you know there's something specific in the flavors between all of them, but you don't quite know what it is, it's cumin. Cumin is the base for taco seasoning, and it's also used in a good deal of Asian cooking as well. You can always use this.

Curry Powder – You can buy store-bought curry powder, or you can make your own once you're a little more advanced in your cooking. Curry powder doesn't typically have the same ingredients in it when you buy from two different places. Generally, you'll find turmeric, coriander, cumin, and cinnamon in curry powders bought at common grocery stores, but you will find other things like fenugreek, mango powder, and cloves in other batches as well. Every household in India has a different mix for their curry powders, so you may need to sample a few and see what you like best!

Dried Basil – Perfect for giving sauces that classic Italian taste.

Dried Oregano – Perfect for making pizza and pasta sauces with that Italian flare you know and love.

Dried Parsley – A popular dried herb that brings a little bit of freshness to the dishes it's used in.

Dried Rosemary – This herb is perfect for poultry and, with a little bit of garlic and lemon, can make a heck of a flavor combination!

Dried Thyme – This herb is a bit earthier and can be used with poultry as well to help make the flavor more rounded.

Garlic Powder – Many home chefs will tell you that it doesn't matter what the dish calls for, they'll double the amount of garlic that's supposed to be in it. Garlic is a classic flavor that can bring life to your dishes.

Ground Black Pepper – This is a classic for any table and should be added to taste in every recipe you cook that isn't sweet.

Honey – Honey can add sweetness to sauces, it's great in tea, and it's ideal to have around the house when you need it.

Onion Powder – This is a great compliment to garlic powder, and it's good if you need a hint of a flavor of onions, but you don't want to cut up a whole onion for your dish. Perfect for seasoning chicken before a bake.

Paprika – There are several different kinds of paprika, but it's a great base to put in your seasoning mixes when you cook. By using paprika, you'll be sure there's a delicious, savory flavor in just about everything you make.

Salt – This is non-negotiable. You must salt your food appropriately, or it will not be good. Too little salt and the food is bland and boring. Too much salt, and it's almost painful to eat. Make sure you're tasting your food as you cook, so you know you're salting your food enough!

Canned and Dry Goods

Condensed Milk – This is used to moisten and thicken recipes while adding a creamy sweetness that doesn't involve too much moisture or work on your part. If a recipe called for sweetened condensed milk, there is little to no substitute.

Evaporated Milk – While being very similar to condensed milk, the major difference is sweetness. Condensed milk is sweetened, while evaporated milk is not.

Dried Fruits – Raisins, figs, apricots, and more are a great ingredient to put into your baked goods.

Nuts – Nuts are used as a great way to add a little bit of crunch to your brownies, a nice topping for croissants, and so much more. Baking without nuts is certainly possible, but you will encounter a lot of recipes containing nuts.

Cold Goods

Eggs – You will often find eggs as a wash or a binding agent in your baked goods, though it is possible to substitute if you prefer not to eat eggs or animal products.

Milk – Many recipes call for the use of milk as a moistener. If you prefer not to use milk with lactose or animal products at all, there are several nut or soy alternatives that are great for baking. Lactose-free milk is another great option as well.

CHAPTER 3: HOW TO MEASURE

In baking more than cooking, you must be familiar with and follow the exact measurements that are laid out in the recipes. Knowing what all the abbreviations for units of measurement will help you to be able to read your recipes and follow them exactly. One of the most classic blunders in cooking is needing 2 teaspoons of something and using 2 tablespoons instead, resulting in an over-salted or over-seasoned mess.

Teaspoon (tsp., t.)

A teaspoon is 1/3 of a tablespoon.

Tablespoon (tbsp., tb.)

A tablespoon is ½ of an ounce.

Gram (g.)

A gram is one-thousandth of a kilogram or about 1/28 of an ounce. This is generally used outside the US for measurements or for very small amounts of ingredients.

Ounce (oz.)

An ounce is 2 tablespoons or 28.3495 grams.

Cup (c.)

A cup is 8 ounces.

Pint (pt.)

A pint is two cups or 16 ounces.

Quart (qt.)

A quart is ¼ of a gallon or 32 ounces.

Gallon (gal.)

A gallon is four quarts or 128 ounces.

Pound (lb.)

A pound is 16 ounces.

You may find that you need to do some math when you're putting together the perfect recipe. If someone tells you that you need ¼ of a cup of something, but the packaging measures it in ounces, you want to make sure that you're getting enough of it, right? So you need to be able to tell that ¼ of a cup is ¼ of 8 ounces, which leaves you with what? 2 ounces.

If you need 6 pints of something, but quarts are on sale at the grocery store, you might be able to save money by buying 3 quarts instead. Or, if a gallon is cheapest, you could just buy that and have a quart leftover for other recipes or other uses.

If you're trying to measure out one ounce of something and you've already used the teaspoon and don't want to dirty another dish, you can know that 6 teaspoons is one ounce since 3 teaspoons equals one tablespoon and 2 tablespoons equals 1 ounce.

Once you get more familiar with measuring quantities of things, you will find it to be easier and easier.

Tip: How to Measure Using a Scale

Some materials and ingredients will need to be weighed with a scale, as those ingredients are measured by weight. Things like meat and flour can be weighed in order to tell you how much you're using or eating.

Many professional bakers prefer to weigh their flour rather than using cups and tablespoons to measure, as it gives you a more accurate picture of what you're adding to the recipe.

If you would like to weigh your ingredients in the kitchen, you will need a kitchen scale. Generally, these are fairly inexpensive and small scales. Digital ones are the easiest to balance and read, but there are certainly analog scales if that's what you prefer. To weigh your ingredients on a digital scale, you'll want to place your bowl or cup on the scale. Something with a wide mouth is best. Turn on the scale to set the tare weight. Tare weight is the weight of the things that are sitting on the scale, which you don't want factored into the final measurement. For instance, if you want to weigh a bowl of raw beans, you don't want the weight of the bowl in that figure. So you put the bowl on the scale first, turn it on and make sure the reading is at zero (there is usually a button to register a new tare weight just in case), and then pour the beans or other ingredients into the bowl for an accurate reading.If a recipe calls for one cup of flour, you want to weigh out 125g or 4.25 oz. It's crucial to make sure you measure out the right amounts of each ingredient, so nothing is out of proportion. You will find this is especially true of baking, whereas cooking can sometimes be a little looser on measurements.

Chapter 4: Baker's Tools

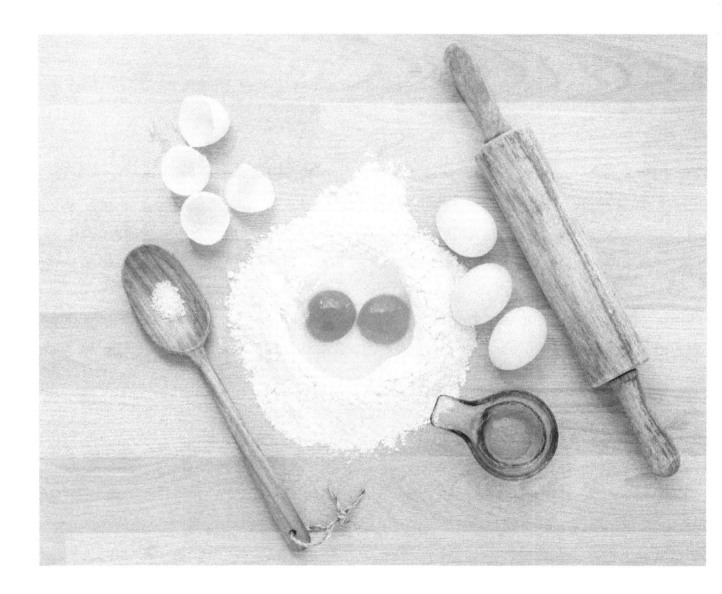

Baking Dishes – There are many dishes that you might want to cook in the oven. A ceramic dish that is deeper than your average cookie sheet or baking pan is the perfect tool for such a job and should be kept on hand if you like to make delicious meals for the whole family in the oven.

Blender – This might be one of the more seldom-used tools, but it's one of those things that you can't really come up with a replacement or substitute for when you're in a pinch and need one, so many chefs like to keep them on hand for when they need them. You can use a blender to even out the texture of a soup or a sauce, you can use it to make a base for something, and it's just the best tool for what it does

Cake Tins – Baking a cake can really only happen in a cake tin. Baked goods take on the shape of the container they're in if they're rising, and you want something that is as uniform as possible.

Can Opener – Opening cans with a sticky or rusty can opener can slow down your whole rhythm when cooking, so it's best to get a can opener that can glide right through and open cans with ease.

Cookie Sheets - These are a classic, and they usually come in packs of three. You will need these for sheet pan recipes as well as cookies.

Cutting Board – Don't cut your meat, fruit, and vegetables on the bare counter, or you'll scuff up the counters and dull your knives! Get a cutting board made of wood, resin, or plastic that will help keep your prep work safe and hygienic.

Food Processor – This might be one of the more seldom-used tools, but it's one of those things that you can't really come up with a replacement or substitute for when you're in a pinch and need one, so many chefs like to keep them on hand for when they need them. You can use a food processor to grind meat, make guacamole, chop up veggies into rough pieces, and so much more.

Grater – A classic cheese grater can be used for so many more things than just cheese. You can use grated things in many different recipes, so don't discount their use.

Hand Mixer – When you're putting together a thick mixture, a hand mixer can mean the difference between five minutes and thirty. When flour starts to bind with liquid and fat, it can get tough, or when potatoes need quick and smooth mashing, it can take a long time. A hand mixer cuts that work in half.

Kitchen Shears – These are large kitchen scissors that are very sharp. They are meant to cut through the thin backbones of chicken, the leaves of an artichoke, and so much more. Kitchen shears can make quick work of a lot of tasks.

Knives – Any chef will tell you that their knives are their most prized tools. A basic chef's knife is a good place to start, and you will find more knives with more uses as you gain experience and get better with them.

Mixing Bowls – Mixing bowls help you to get a batter or a dough together in the right amounts. Other bowls in the kitchen just aren't big enough.

Paring Knife – This will help you to make small decorative cuts in your pastry or to make the small, precise cuts needed on some baked goods.

Pie Pans – When you're making a pie, nothing is quite like a pie pan, as it's got slanted edges that make it nice and easy for the delicate crust to form.

Rolling Mat – While these aren't completely essential, it is nice to have a rolling mat for easy cleanup, as well as to tell you how big your dough is.

Rolling Pin – You can use other things in the kitchen to roll out your dough, but at the end of the day, the rolling pin is just the best tool for the job. Don't forget to flour it!

Rubber Spatulas – Rubber or silicone spatulas are helpful because they make complete contact with the side of the bowl and can completely scrape all the batter or contents out for you. It makes washing those big mixing bowls so much easier!

Saucepan – A medium saucepan will be called for in a large number of recipes that you'll find.

Spatula – Every chef needs a spatula! You can't even cook an egg or get your cookies off the cookie sheet without a spatula, so this is one of the very bare basics every chef needs.

Strainer – Whether you choose to go with a fine-mesh sieve or colander, you will need a way to remove water or liquid from your dishes at some point or another. Colanders are typically used for draining pasta, and sieves are used for rinsing rice before cooking, but both have many uses.

Thermometer – A meat thermometer or kitchen thermometer can tell you how far along your cooking is coming and how soon you will need to pull things off or out of the heat.

Timer – Most chefs will need a reminder when their time is up for things that are being cooked, especially if it's in the oven. Out of sight, out of mind, and you don't want your food in the oven to go out of mind!

Tongs – These are a precision tool that allows you to pick things up and flip or move them with ease. These can help you to do a lot of things and make the kitchen work a lot easier.

Vegetable Peeler – Whether you're peeling carrots, potatoes, apples, or something else, these make that work so much easier. Pros can use paring knives; peelers are much more precise and faster.

Whisk – A whisk can sometimes be substituted for a fork, but a good whisk can help you whip up things that a fork generally can't. This tool is found at most chef's stations.

Zester – You can't really zest with any other tool in your kitchen with the exception of maybe the paring knife and the grater. A zester is far faster and easier to use, though, so that is more highly recommended.

CHAPTER 5: PREPARING YOUR TABLE

When you're getting ready to bake, the first thing you want to do is make sure that your table, counter, or workspace is completely clear. You don't want to be moving things, washing dishes, and digging through the cabinets for the ingredients you need while you're in the middle of baking unless you have the downtime to do so.

Here's a little checklist that you can use to make sure that you've gotten all your tasks lined up in just the right way, so your baking process goes as smoothly as possible!

1. Have all the dishes I will need been washed and dried already?
2. Is the sink clear of dirty dishes, so I won't need to wash or move them while I'm trying to bake?
3. Have all my tools been cleaned, dried, and laid out for me to use?
4. Have all my ingredients been laid out so I can access them easily?
5. Do I have all the seasonings and condiments that I will need in order to make my creation delicious?
6. Have I set my oven to preheat at the right temperature?

Going down this checklist and making sure that you've gotten everything you need is a great way to save yourself a lot of time in the kitchen. There are few things worse than being at a critical stage when you need to add an ingredient, only to find that you don't have it laid out in front of you. This means that you need to run and find the ingredient and hope that nothing got messed up when you were looking. In many cases, when you're baking, your hands will be covered with butter, flour, oil, or some other mess and you will need to pay your way through the cabinets with greasy fingers, or wash your hands and start all over again on your mixing once you've got the ingredients that you need.

Making sure that you have everything you need doesn't need to look like it does on cooking shows. You don't need a hundred little bowls with all your ingredients in them laid out before you, and you don't need to use every dish in the house just to bake. If this works for you and you prefer to do things this way, that is perfectly fine.

One piece of advice that can help you if you're choosing to run your kitchen in this way is to wash dishes as you go. You will reach certain stages in the baking process when your dough needs to rest or when your creation is in the oven. When you're waiting for things like this, go ahead and rinse or wash your dishes and clean your sink out. You will find that if you decide not to do this, your kitchen will look like a whole bag of flour exploded in the middle of it and took every dish in the kitchen along with it. Taking five minutes while your creations are rising or baking can make a world of difference at the end of your labors when your creation is golden brown and delicious, and the kitchen is spotless in spite of all that went on in there.

Preparation is key when you're working in the kitchen, but so is leaving the kitchen the way you found it. If you don't own the home you're baking in; it can make your parents or the people who live in your home feel like they're being crowded with lots of dirty dishes. If you wash as you go, you won't feel like the dishes take very long at all!

Chapter 6: Breakfast Baking Recipes

Dutch Baby

A Dutch Baby is essentially a giant pancake but with a flair and style that the pancake lacks.

The ingredients you will need are as follows:

★ A half-cup of flour

★ A quarter teaspoon of salt

★ 2 eggs

★ A single teaspoon of vanilla

★ A single lemon

★ 3 tablespoons of butter that is unsalted

★ A single tablespoon of sugar

★ A single cup of milk

★ A single tablespoon of powdered sugar garnish for the dish

The steps you will need to complete are as follows:

1. Make sure that your oven is preheated to 400 degrees F.
2. Get yourself a bowl.
3. Get a whisk.
4. You will need to use the whisk and whisk the milk and flour together until it has become smooth and then add in your eggs along with your vanilla, sugar, and salt.
5. Whisk them all together and make sure they combine before setting them aside.
6. Get a skillet that is safe for the oven.
7. Place the butter in the skillet.
8. Put the skillet in the oven after making sure that you have preheated it in step

9.	Watch the pan very closely and make sure that when the butter is sizzling that you pour batter into your pan.

10.	Shut the door and do not open it.

11.	Allow your Dutch Baby to cook for 17 minutes.

12.	Remove from the oven and garnish with powdered sugar.

13.	Cut into it however you like, and it's ready for you to eat.

This recipe is able to give you 6 slices.

You will need half an hour to prep and cook this dish.

Nutritional information (per serving):

➢	Calories-140

➢	Fat-8 grams

➢	Carbs-12 grams

➢	Protein-5 grams

➢	Fiber-1 gram

Quiche

Quiche is a great meal that is easy to make and will yield a lot of leftovers. It's great for meal planning and testing your abilities as a chef. Many consider it to be a meal of formal occasions, but these days everyone makes them.

The ingredients you will need for this recipe are as follows:

★   A half teaspoon of salt

★   A single cup of shredded cheese (use cheddar)

★   A quarter teaspoon of pepper

★   A whole wheat pie crust that measures 9 inches

★   ¾ of a cup of milk (use whole milk)

★   5 eggs (large)

★   2 cups of florets of broccoli

The steps you will need to complete this dish are as follows:

1.   Make sure that your oven has been preheated to 375 degrees F.

2.   Roll out your crust if it doesn't have a shape.

3.   Chill the crust until you need to use it.

4.   Get a small pot.

5.   Place a minimum of one cups of water and a maximum of two cups of water into the bottom of the pot.

6.   Add in your broccoli and then cover your pot.

7.   Bring to a boil.

8.   Cook your broccoli until it is tender and crispy. This will take 4 minutes.

9.   Move your broccoli from the pot to a colander.

10.   Rinse with cool water and make sure it drains thoroughly.

11.   Carefully chop broccoli into pieces that are small.

12.   Get a large bowl.

13.   Get a whisk.

14. In the bowl, you will need to whisk together your milk, pepper, and salt, along with your eggs.

15. Get your broccoli and stir it in along with the cheese.

16. Pour mixture into the pie shell that has been prepared.

17. Bake the quiche for a minimum of 35 minutes and a maximum of 40 minutes. The eggs should be set in the middle.

18. You should check on the quiche at the 25-minute mark. If you notice that the crust is browning too quickly, you will need to tent it with foil.

19. Let it stand for a solid 5 minutes before you serve it.

This recipe will give you 8 servings.

It will take you 55 minutes to prep and cook this recipe.

Nutritional information:

This is based upon a serving. The serving size for this recipe is ⅛ of the quiche.

- ➢ Calories-228
- ➢ Fat-16 grams
- ➢ Carbs-12 grams
- ➢ Protein-10 grams
- ➢ Fiber-2 grams

Blueberry Swirl Muffins

Muffins are a staple for breakfasts, and they make a tasty snack for other parts of the day as well. As a chef adding muffins to your arsenal is a must.

The ingredients you will need for this recipe are as follows.

For the muffins themselves:
- ★ 2 and a half cups of flour (use all-purpose)
- ★ 2 cups of divided blueberries
- ★ A single teaspoon of granulated sugar
- ★ 2 eggs (use large)
- ★ 4 tablespoons of butter that is unsalted and has been melted and cooled
- ★ A quarter cup of vegetable oil
- ★ A single cup of buttermilk
- ★ A cup and ⅛ of granulated sugar
- ★ 2 and a half teaspoons of baking powder
- ★ A single teaspoon of table salt
- ★ A teaspoon and a half of vanilla extract

For the topping:
- ★ A teaspoon and a half of grated lemon zest
- ★ A third of a cup of granulated sugar

The steps you will need to complete this recipe are as follows.
1. Adjust one of the oven racks to an upper-middle position, and be sure to heat your oven to 425.
2. Get yourself a cupcake pan with a dozen cups.
3. Line the pan.
4. Set your pan to the side.

5.   Get a saucepan.

6.   Add in a single teaspoon of sugar along with a single cup of blueberries and bring to a simmer. The heat should be set to medium to accomplish this.

7.   Smash your berries until they have thickened and reduced to a quarter cup about 6 minutes.

8.   Get a small bowl and place the mix in it.

9.   Let cool for a quarter of an hour.

10.   Get a large bowl.

11.   Get a whisk.

12.   Use the whisk and whisk the salt, flour, and baking powder together.

13.   Get a smaller bowl that is of medium size.

14.   Use the whisk again on the eggs and remaining sugar and whisk them until combined and nice and thick.

15.   Whisk in the butter but do this slowly and whisk in the oil slowly until they too have combined.

16.   Whisk in the vanilla and buttermilk as well until they have combined.

17.   Get a spatula made of rubber.

18.   Fold the egg mixture in and the remaining berries to the flour mixture until moistened.

19.   It is important that you don't over mix here. You want the batter lumpy in a few spots and have a few spots of dry flour remaining as well.

20.   Use a spoon and place the batter in the prepared cupcake pan.

21.   Fill the cups completely and mound slightly.

22.   Place a teaspoon of the berry mix you cooked to the center of each cup.

23.   Use a toothpick to give it the swirl design.

24.   Sprinkle the topping you made over the top.

25.   Bake for 18 minutes. The muffins should be a golden brown, and if you shove a toothpick in the middle, it should come out clean or with very few moist crumbs attached.

26.   It helps to rotate the pan at the halfway mark.

27.   Let cool for 5 minutes and place on a wire rack for an additional 5 minutes of cooling.

This recipe will give you a dozen muffins.

You will need an hour to complete this dish.

Nutritional information (per serving):

- ➢   Calories-293
- ➢   Fat- 9 grams
- ➢   Carbs-49 grams
- ➢   Protein-4 grams
- ➢   Fiber- 1 gram

Cinnamon Buns

Cinnamon buns should be a decadent and delicious meal that makes you feel like you have just had dessert.

The ingredients you will need for this recipe is as follows:

How to make the icing:
- ★ A single cup of sugar that is powdered
- ★ 4 ounces of room temperature cream cheese
- ★ 2 tablespoons of milk
- ★ A single teaspoon of vanilla extract that is pure
- ★ 2 tablespoons of butter that has been melted

For the rolls themselves:
- ★ A single egg (use large) that will be lightly whisked
- ★ Cooking oil spray
- ★ A quarter of a teaspoon of salt
- ★ 3 and a half cups of all-purpose flour

For the yeast:
- ★ A single cup of milk that has been warmed to the touch. Do not make it hot.
- ★ 2 and a half teaspoons of yeast that is a quick rise
- ★ 5 tablespoons of sugar that is granulated
- ★ A quarter of a cup of butter that has been melted

For the filling:
- ★ 2 tablespoons of butter that has been melted
- ★ half a cup of brown sugar that has been loosely packed
- ★ 2 tablespoons of cinnamon (you will need to use ground in this case)

The steps you will need to complete this recipe are as follows:

1. Heat your oven to 200 F.

For the yeast:

1. Get a large bowl.
2. Combine the butter that is melted, with the warm milk and yeast as well as the sugar.
3. It will need to stand for 10 minutes. It should appear frothy.

For the rolls:

1. Add the whisked egg from the ingredients list to the milk mixture. Add in 3 and a half cups of flour. No more, no less. You will have a soft but sticky dough
2. Use flat and lightly floured surface to turn the dough out.
3. You will need to knead the dough until it is both elastic and smooth at the same time. It will take 2 minutes to accomplish this.
4. Get a large bowl.
5. Coat the bowl lightly with the spray and transfer your dough to the bowl.
6. Make sure that the dough is coated in the oil.
7. Cover with a towel that is damp.
8. Turn your oven off, but transfer the bowl of dough into the oven while it's warm.
9. If you see an indention, that means the dough has not been able to raise enough. It should take a half-hour for the dough to rise.
10. Punch your dough down, then cover, and then you will need to let the dough rest for another half hour. The dough's size should be doubled.
11. Roll out the dough onto a floured surface and into a 19 inch by 13-inch rectangle.
12. Brush the butter that has been melted over your dough and then sprinkle the dough with cinnamon and brown sugar.
13. Rub the cinnamon mix into your butter, but make sure that you are gentle about it.

14.   At one side, that is long and roll up your dough tightly like a roll.

15.   Pinch (gently) on the seam to make sure that it will seal.

16.   Trim off the ends for the slices and cut the dough so it will make a dozen rolls.

17.   Grease a baking dish that is 9 by 13 lightly and arrange the rolls you made.

18.   You will need to cover this with a damp towel and allow it to rise for a half-hour.

19.   While it's doing this, heat the oven to 350 F.

20.   Uncover your rolls and then bake for 25 minutes. They should look golden brown. Make sure that they have cooled slightly before you attempt to glaze them.

Now for the icing:

1.   Prepare the icing while your rolls are in the oven. Beat together the vanilla, cream cheese, and butter until they have become both creamy and smooth.

2.   Beat in your powdered sugar until there are no lumps whatsoever.

3.   Spread the icing on top.

This recipe will give you a dozen rolls.

It will take you 2 hours and an additional 15 minutes to complete this recipe.

Nutritional information (per serving):
➤   Calories-322
➤   Carbs-46 grams
➤   Protein-6 grams
➤   Fat-12 grams
➤   Fiber-1 gram

Bacon Cheese Bread

Bacon cheese bread is both delicious and filling and leaves you completely satisfied. It is great for parties or when you feel like something savory for yourself.

The ingredients that you will need for this recipe are as follows:
- ★ A loaf of french bread that is 14 ounces
- ★ A single tablespoon of dip mix (go with ranch)
- ★ ¾ of a cup of mayonnaise
- ★ 2 cups of cheese that has been shredded
- ★ 4 slices of baked bacon that has been crumbled

The steps you will need to follow to complete this recipe are as follows:
1. Preheat your broiler.
2. Cut your bread in half (do this lengthwise).
3. Line your baking sheet with a foil that is nonstick.
4. Get a bowl.
5. Combine your bacon, cheese, mayo, and ranch in the bowl.
6. Use a spatula to spread your cheese on both halves of the bread.
7. Place under your broiler for 8 minutes until it turns a golden brown.
8. Before you cut it, let it cool slightly.

This recipe will give you 20 servings.

You will need fifteen minutes to complete this dish.

Nutritional information (per serving)::
- ➢ Calories-168
- ➢ Carbs-11 grams
- ➢ Protein-5 grams
- ➢ Fat- 10 grams

Popovers

Popovers are a great treat, and most of the time, people eat them with jam, but this is a dish that you can get really creative with. This recipe, for example, is for a cheesy popover.

The ingredients that you will need for this recipe are as follows.

★   A single cup of warm milk

★   2 eggs (large)

★   A quarter of a teaspoon of salt

★   A half teaspoon of black pepper (use cracked)

★   3 tablespoons of butter that has been melted

★   A single cup of flour (use all-purpose)

★   2 tablespoons of parmesan (grated finely) and add a little for the top of the popover

The steps you will need to complete this recipe are as follows:

1.   Make sure your oven is preheated to 425 F.

2.   Place a muffin pan inside as it preheats.

3.   Get a bowl.

4.   Get a whisk.

5.   In the bowl, whisk your parmesan, spices, eggs, and milk together.

6.   Add in your flour and mix it just enough so that the lumps are gone.

7.   When your oven is at the appropriate temperature, get your muffin pan (carefully, don't burn yourself), and brush 8 of the spots with your butter that you melted. (if your pan only has 8 spots then you will need to do this again to make another four for a full dozen)

8.   Scoop enough batter into each spot so that it reaches almost the top of your pan.

9.   Sprinkle cheese on top.

10.   Put the pan in the oven.

11.   Bake 20 minutes and turn down your heat to 350 before baking an additiona
ten minutes.

12.   You can serve right away.

This dish will give you a dozen popovers.

You will need 40 minutes to complete this recipe.

Nutritional information (per serving):

➢   Calories-75

Huevos Rancheros

Huevos Rancheros is a wonderful dish that is both cultural and delicious at the same time. Recipes for this meal have flavors that explode on the tongue, and ours is no different. The ingredients that you will need for this recipe are as follows:

- ★ 10 eggs (large)
- ★ half a cup of queso fresco that has been crumbled
- ★ 2 avocados ripe and sliced
- ★ 10 flour tortillas (we recommend Old El Paso)
- ★ 2 tablespoons of oil (vegetable)
- ★ 15 ounces of black beans
- ★ 15 ounces of chorizo (use Mexican)
- ★ Ranchero Sauce

You can also add extra ingredients if you like, but you should be aware of the fact that it will change the nutritional information.

The steps you need to complete the dish are as follows:

1. Warm your sauce on your stove.

2. Pour your beans in a pot that is small (a saucepan is a good option here).

3. Your heat should be medium when you are warming this, and you need to heat until simmering before turning the heat off.

4. Get a skillet that is nonstick and large in size and put the chorizo inside it.

5. Set the heat to medium-high.

6. Break the chorizo apart and then brown it. This should take about ten minutes.

7. Your chorizo should be starting to be crispy, and you will need to put it on a plate.

8. Wipe your skillet down (a paper towel is fine)

9. Add 2 tablespoons of the oil and set it back over that same medium-high heat that you had before.

10.   Add your tortillas a single one at a time. You want them to puff for about 5 seconds before you flip them and then repeat the process.

11.   After you do this, remove the tortillas and then set them on paper towels to drain. Repeat this process until all of your tortillas are golden and puffy.

12.   In the same skillet, you cooked everything else in and cooked the eggs 'to order.'

13.   Place the ingredients on the tortilla.

This recipe will give you 5 servings.

You will need 25 minutes to complete this dish.

Nutritional information (per serving):

➢   Calories-1019

➢   Carbs-60 grams

➢   Protein-47 grams

➢   Fat-65 grams

➢   Fiber-14 grams

Breakfast Pizza

Love pizza? Then you'll love this! It's the perfect starter to your day.

The ingredients you will need for this recipe are as follows:

★   A single handful of spinach (use baby spinach)

★   8 sliced cherry tomatoes

★   4 eggs that are large

★   A single cup and 5 ounces of all-purpose flour (you can also use white whole wheat flour)

★   2 strips of chopped and cooked center cut bacon

★   2 ounces and a half cup of mozzarella cheese (shredded)

★   Half a teaspoon of salt (kosher)

★   A teaspoon and a half of baking powder

★   A single cup of Greek yogurt (use nonfat and make sure it has no liquid)

The steps that you will need to complete this recipe are as follows:

1.   Make sure that your oven is preheated to 450 F.

2.   Get a baking sheet and place a silicone liner on it.

3.   Get a bowl.

4.   Combine your salt and baking powder along with the flour and whisk them together well.

5.   Add in your yogurt and use a fork to mix it. It should be combined well, and you should be able to see small crumbles in the mix.

6.   Dust flour lightly on a flat surface and then remove your dough from the bowl.

7.   Knead the dough for almost 2 dozen turns. Your dough should be tacky and not leave anything on your hand.

8.   Separate the dough into four balls.

9.   Sprinkle the flat surface with flour and do the same to a rolling pin.

10.   Roll until you have an oval that is 8 inches in its diameter.

11.   Place on baking sheet.

12.   Top with cheese, and your spinach, as well as your tomatoes, but leave a hole in the middle open. This is where you're going to put the egg.

13.   Break an egg and place it in the middle of the dough (gentle when you break) and then put the bacon on top.

14.   Bake for 12 minutes. Your crust should be golden. The egg should be set.

15.   Season the dish.

This recipe will give you 4 servings.

This recipe will take you half an hour to complete the recipe.

Nutritional Information (per serving):

➢   Calories-271
➢   Carbs-27 grams
➢   Protein-20.5 grams
➢   Fiber-1.5 grams
➢   Fat-9 grams

Breakfast Casserole

Breakfast casserole is another dish that is easy to make, good for practicing, and makes plenty of food.

The ingredients you will need for this recipe is as follows:

- ★ Half of a teaspoon of pepper
- ★ 2 cups of milk
- ★ 2 pounds of breakfast sausage (hot)
- ★ 8 eggs
- ★ 2 cups of cheddar cheese that is shredded
- ★ A single bag of shredded hash browns that are frozen and 30 ounces

The steps you will need to complete this dish are as follows:

1. Make sure that your oven is preheated to 350.
2. Get a large skillet.
3. Cook the sausage until there is no pink anywhere to be found.
4. Drain your fat.
5. Add your hash browns to your skillet and cook them until they have turned slightly brown.
6. Place those hash browns in a pan that is 9 by 13 and greased lightly.
7. Place your sausage and cheese over the top.
8. Get a whisk.
9. Whisk together your spices, milk, and eggs.
10. Pour this over the top of the other ingredients in the pan.
11. Bake for 40 minutes.

This recipe will give you a dozen servings.
This recipe will need 45 minutes to complete.

Nutritional information (per serving):

- ➢ Calories-632
- ➢ Fat-46 grams
- ➢ Carbs-26 grams
- ➢ Fiber- 3 grams
- ➢ Protein-24 grams

Flaky Buttermilk Biscuits

Buttermilk biscuits are a staple in most homes. Particularly in certain cuisines. This recipe is a good one to have your disposal as a chef.

The ingredients that you will need for your dish are as follows:

★   A single cup of buttermilk

★   3 cups of flour that is all-purpose

★   4 teaspoons of sugar

★   A single teaspoon and a half of salt (kosher)

★   8 teaspoons of baking powder

★   A dozen tablespoons of butter (this amounts to a stick and a half). They will need to be cut into pieces that are half an inch and chilled.

The steps you will need to complete for this dish are as follows:

1.   Get a bowl.

2.   Combine your sugar and salt with your flour and baking powder.

3.   Get a whisk.

4.   Whisk these items together until you find that the mixture has combined well.

5.   Add the pieces of butter that you sliced.

6.   Use your fingers and rub the flour mix together until half of the butter has combined thoroughly. The remaining half should be in small pieces and some bigger sized pieces, but none should be bigger than a hazelnut.

7.   Add in your buttermilk.

8.   Mix it together with a spatula and do this until the dry ingredients have just moistened.

9.   Add in additional milk if needed but do it one tablespoon at a time.

10.   On a flat surface, lightly dust your space with flour, then place your dough on it and press it until it forms a rectangle.

11.   Fold this in half and turn the dough 90 degrees.

12. Flatten it again.

13. Repeat this process until you have four.

14. You will know when it's the proper look when it is fairly smooth.

15. Roll your dough until it is a quarter-inch thick.

16. Get a biscuit cutter.

17. Use it to cut as many biscuits as possible.

18. Place these biscuits on a sheet pan that has been lined with parchment.

19. Place the pan in the fridge for a half-hour.

20. Use the extra dough to make more biscuits (the scraps).

21.   Heat your oven to 350 F.

22. When the biscuits are done in the fridge and put them in the oven.

23. Bake for 20 minutes. The bottoms should be golden brown and firm.

This recipe will yield you 18 biscuits.

It will take you an hour and 5 minutes to complete this dish.

Nutritional information (per serving):

➢   Calories-165

➢   Fat-9 grams

➢   Protein-2 grams

➢   Carbs-18 grams

CHAPTER 7: MAIN COURSE BAKING RECIPES

Roasted Whole Chicken with Root Vegetables

Nutritious and delicious. This is a great dish for any chef to learn and become familiar with.

The ingredients you will need for this recipe are as follows:

★　　A whole chicken (four pounds)

★　　2 tablespoons of fresh rosemary (you need it to be finely chopped and an additional three sprigs for the cavity)

★　　A single tablespoon of fresh sage (chopped and four additional sprigs for the cavity)

★　　A single teaspoon and a half of red pepper flakes

★　　6 tablespoons of olive oil

★　　2 tablespoons of fresh thyme (chopped finely and 3 additional sprigs for the cavity)

★　　4 carrots (slender and peeled)

★　　The zest of a single lemon and a half of a lemon

★　　2 garlic cloves that are grated finely (you need the remaining head of garlic, and you will need to halve it in a horizontal manner to expose the cloves in each half)

★　　2 bay leaves

★　　A single turnip that is medium in size (you need to peel it and cut it into ¾ inch pieces)

★　　A single pound of rutabaga (peel it and cut it into ¾ inch pieces. Cubes will look aesthetically pleasing. Don't eat or use the leaves at all)

The steps you will need to complete this dish are as follows:

1.　　Make sure your oven is preheated to 375 F.

2.　　Place your chicken on a baking pan that is rimmed.

3.　　Get a small bowl.

4.   Place the pepper flakes, garlic, zest, rosemary, sage, thyme, oil, a single teaspoon of salt, and two of the pepper in the bowl. Stir everything to make sure that it is combining.

5.   Rub your chicken completely with half of the herb oil. Make sure that you get some under the skin of the thighs and breasts.

6.   Stuff the cavity with your sprigs of thyme, rosemary, and sage, along with your bay leaves, half lemon and garlic head halves that you made.

7.   Place your veggies in a bowl.

8.   Toss the veggies in the remaining oil mixture.

9.   Place the veggies around the chicken and put it in the oven.

10.   Roast until the vegetables have become tender, and the chicken has been cooked through. You will be able to tell it's done with a thermometer that is instant read and insert it into the thickest part of the thigh. It should read 160 degrees F a around the time of an hour and 15 minutes.

11.   Let it sit for 10 minutes before you carve it.

This recipe will give you 8 servings.

You will need 2 and a half hours to complete this dish.

Nutritional Information (per serving):
- ➤   Calories-564
- ➤   Fiber-3 grams
- ➤   Fat-35 grams
- ➤   Protein-51 grams
- ➤   Carbs-12 grams

Chicken Pot Pie

Chicken pot pie is a classic, and it's been around forever. Many find it comforting and makes people happy when they eat it.

The ingredients that you will need for this dish are as follows:

- ★ A single teaspoon of thyme (dried)
- ★ A single cup of cubed butter
- ★ 2 cups of potatoes that are peeled and diced
- ★ ⅔ of a cup of onion that is chopped
- ★ A single cup of peas that are frozen
- ★ A cup of corn that is frozen
- ★ 3 cups of chicken broth
- ★ A single cup of all-purpose flour
- ★ A single cup and ¾ of carrots that are sliced
- ★ 4 sheets of pie crust (refrigerated)
- ★ ¾ teaspoon of pepper
- ★ A single teaspoon and ¾ of salt
- ★ A single cup and a half of whole milk
- ★ 4 cups of chicken (cooked and cubed)

The steps you will need for this dish are as follows:

1. Make sure that your oven is preheated to 425.
2. Place your carrots and potatoes in a saucepan.
3. You will need to add water to cover.
4. Bring it to a boil.
5. Reduce your heat and then cover and cook for 10 minutes.
6. They should be tender and crispy.
7. Drain.

8. Get a large skillet.

9. Heat your butter over a heat that is medium-high.

10. Add in the onion and cook it until it's tender. Don't forget to stir.

11. Stir in the seasonings and the flour until it has blended.

12. Slowly stir in your milk and broth before bringing it to a boil. Stir constantly here.

13. Cook and stir it for an additional 2 minutes.

14. It should be thickened now.

15. Stir in your potato, corn, chicken, and peas mix and remove from the heat.

16. Unroll your pie crust into a 9-inch pie plate. Trim, so it's even with the rim of the plate.

17. Add in the chicken mix.

18. Unroll the other crusts and place over your filling.

19. Trim it and seal it.

20. Flute the edges.

21. Cut slits in the tops.

22. Bake for 40 minutes, and you should see a crust that is lightly browned.

23. Let it stand for a quarter of an hour before you cut it.

This recipe will make 2 pot pies at eight servings each.

You will need an hour and 15 minutes to complete this dish.

Nutritional information (per serving):

➢ Calories-475

➢ Fat-28 grams

➢ Carbs-41 grams

➢ Protein-15 grams

➢ Fiber- 2 grams

Baked Ziti

Savory and very filling this is another dish that is a good start for becoming a great chef.

The ingredients you will need for this recipe is as follows:

- ★ A single onion that has been chopped
- ★ 2 jars of spaghetti sauce (26-ounce jars)
- ★ A single pound of ziti pasta (dry)
- ★ A single pound of ground beef that is lean
- ★ A single cup and a half of sour cream
- ★ 2 tablespoons of parmesan cheese that is grated
- ★ 6 ounces of provolone cheese that has been sliced
- ★ 6 ounces of mozzarella cheese that has been shredded

The steps to complete this dish are as follows:

1. Get a large pot.
2. Bring a pot of water that has been lightly salted to a boil.
3. Add pasta and cook till al dente. This is approximately 8 minutes.
4. Drain it.
5. Get a skillet.
6. In the skillet brown the beef and onion over a heat of medium.
7. Add the sauce and simmer for a quarter of an hour.
8. Preheat your oven to 350.
9. Get a baking dish that is 9 by 13.
10. Butter the baking dish.
11. Layer the dish with half of the ziti, provolone cheese, sour cream, half of the sauce mix, the remaining ziti and then the mozzarella and the rest of the sauce.
12. Top with the parmesan.
13. Bake a half-hour, and the cheese should be melted.

This recipe will take you an hour to complete.

Nutritional information (per serving):

- ➢   Calories-578
- ➢   Fat-25.3 grams
- ➢   Carbs-58.4 grams
- ➢   Protein-27.9 grams

Shepherd's Pie

The ingredients that you will need for this recipe is as follows:

- ★ A single tablespoon of butter
- ★ A single tablespoon of onion that has been chopped finely
- ★ 4 potatoes that are cubed, peeled and large in size
- ★ A quarter cup of cheddar cheese that has been shredded
- ★ 5 chopped carrots
- ★ A single chopped onion
- ★ A single pound of ground beef that is lean
- ★ 2 tablespoons of flour (use all-purpose)
- ★ A single tablespoon of vegetable oil
- ★ A single tablespoon of ketchup
- ★ A quarter cup of cheddar cheese that is shredded
- ★ ¾ of a cup of broth that is beef

The steps needed for this dish are as follows:

1. Get a large pot and add salted water to it before bringing it to a boil.
2. Add your potatoes and cook them until they are firm but tender. This should take a quarter of an hour.
3. Drain it before mashing it.
4. Mix in your butter and the onion that is finely chopped along with a quarter cup of the cheese that is shredded.
5. Season and place to the side.
6. Bring a large pot of water that has been salted to a boil and add your carrots. Cook them for a quarter of an hour until firm but tender.
7. Drain and mash them before setting aside.
8. Heat your oven to 375 F.
9. Heat your oil in a frying pan.
10. Add your onion and cook it until it's clear.

11.   Add beef and cook until it has been browned well.

12.   Pour off that excess fat and stir in your flour.

13.   Cook for 60 seconds.

14.   Add your ketchup and then your broth.

15.   Bring to a boil and then reduce your heat and simmer for 5 minutes.

16.   Get a casserole dish (2 quart).

17.   Spread the beef in a layer before adding the carrots and potatoes.

18.   Place your cheese on top.

19.   Bake for 20 minutes. It should have a golden brown color.

This recipe will take an hour to complete.

Nutritional information (per serving):

➢   Calories-452

➢   Fat-17 grams

➢   Carbs-52.5 grams

Baked Macaroni and Cheese

The ingredients that you will need for this recipe are as follows:

- ★   A quarter of a teaspoon of mustard (ground)
- ★   A single tablespoon and a half of butter that has been cut into small pieces
- ★   2 cups of milk that is low fat
- ★   A single pound of sharp shredded cheddar cheese
- ★   A single package of elbow macaroni
- ★   2 tablespoons of flour that is all-purpose
- ★   A quarter teaspoon of salt
- ★   A quarter of a teaspoon of black pepper

The steps that you will need to complete for this recipe are the following:

1. Have an oven that is preheated to 375 F.
2. Get a 9 by 13 casserole dish.
3. Stay the dish.
4. Cook the macaroni, When it's tender, drain it.
5. When the pasta is cooking, combine the 2 and a half cups of cheese with the mustard, flour, and pepper.
6. Get a bowl and combine the cheese mix you just made with the hot pasta and stir it to combine.
7. Pour into the pan.
8. Pour your milk over the pasta.
9. Top the dish with cheese.
10. Dot with butter.
11. Cover with aluminum foil.
12. Bake for 45 minutes. If you choose to, you can take the foil off at the half-hour mark.
13. It should be firm and a brownish golden color.

14.   If you let it sit for 10 minutes before serving, you should be able to let it firm up further.

This recipe will give you six servings.
You will need 90 minutes for this recipe.

Nutritional information (per serving):
  - ➢   Calories-220
  - ➢   Fat- 6 grams
  - ➢   Carbs-34 grams
  - ➢   Protein-10 grams
  - ➢   Fiber-5 grams

Lasagna

This recipe needs the following ingredients:

★   A single pound of beef that is ground and lean

★   32 ounces of cottage cheese

★   A single jar of spaghetti sauce (32 ounces)

★   2 eggs

★   2 teaspoons of parsley (dried)

★   Half a cup of grated parmesan cheese

★   3 cups of mozzarella cheese that is shredded

★   9 lasagna noodles

★   Half a cup of water

The steps you need to complete this dish are the following:

1. Get a large skillet.

2. Put your heat to medium.

3. Brown your ground beef before draining all the grease.

4. Add the sauce and simmer for 5 minutes.

5. Get a bowl.

6. Mix together mozzarella cheese (leave one cup out), eggs,cottage cheese, spices, and half of the parmesan cheese.

7. Get a baking dish that is 9 by 13.

8. Spread ¾ of the sauce mix in the pan and then place 3 lasagna noodles (uncooked) over it.

9. Then place the remaining mozzarella and parmesan cheese.

10. Add half a cup of water to your edges of the pan.

11. Cover with your aluminum foil.

12. Heat your oven to 350 F.

13. Bake for 45 minutes.

14. Uncover your dish.

15. Bake ten more minutes.

16. Let it stand for ten minutes; then it's ready.

This recipe will take an hour and a half to complete.

Nutritional information (per serving):

➢ Calories-377

➢ Fat-26.4 grams

➢ Carbs-26.4 grams

➢ Protein-29.4 grams

Pizza

The ingredients that you will need for this recipe is as follows:

- ★   A single pound and a half of pizza dough
- ★   A single cup of basil leaves that are torn and fresh
- ★   8 ounces of sliced mozzarella cheese
- ★   28 ounce can of tomatoes that are whole, peeled and drained
- ★   4 large minced garlic cloves

The steps needed for this dish are the following:

1. Heat your oven to 450 degrees.
2. If you choose to use a pizza stone in the oven to warm.
3. Roll out your dough on a surface that is lightly floured.
4. Press into a large circle gently and make sure that it is a quarter-inch thick.

For the sauce:

1. Get a bowl.
2. Hand crush the tomatoes in the bowl.
3. Add garlic and spices (salt and pepper) in the bowl and stir it before placing it to the side.
4. Place the sauce on the dough and then add cheese and half of the basil.

Last instructions:

1. Bake for 25 minutes until the cheese is bubbling and the crust is golden in color. Place the rest of the basil on top.

Nutritional information (per serving, 2 slices):

- ➢   Calories-390
- ➢   Fat-11 grams

➢ Carbs- 52 grams

➢ Protein-15 grams

➢ Fiber- 3 grams

Meatloaf

The ingredients that you need are as follows:

★   Half a teaspoon of both salt and pepper (ground pepper)

★   Half a cup of diced onion

★   A single egg

★   A single cup of grated parmesan cheese

★   16 ounces of ground beef that is 90% grass-fed and lean

★   A quarter of a cup of ketchup

★   A third of a cup of ketchup

The steps for the recipe that you will need to do are the following:

1.   Heat the oven to 350 F.

2.   Get a loaf pan.

3.   Line it with aluminum foil.

4.   Dice the onion finely.

5.   Mix all of your ingredients in a bowl except for the last third of a cup of ketchup. Either use your hands or something to stir it.

6.   Form it into a loaf and stick it in the pan topping it with the rest of the ketchup.

7.   Bake for 60 minutes.

8.   When finished, let stand for 5 minutes.

This recipe will give you 4 servings

This recipe will take you an hour and 10 minutes to complete

Nutritional information (per serving):

➢   Calories-342

➢   Fat-17.5 grams

➢   Protein-36.2 grams

➢ Carbs-9.6 grams

Chicken Fiesta Bake

The ingredients for this recipe are as follows:

- ★ 2-3 chicken breasts that have been sliced width wise in half
- ★ Taco seasoning
- ★ Half a cup of medium cheddar cheese
- ★ Diced green onion
- ★ A single 16 ounce of salsa (medium)
- ★ A single can of undrained corn
- ★ A cup of rice that is white and long grain
- ★ A third of a cup of water
- ★ A single can of drained and rinsed black beans

The steps to complete this recipe are as follows:

1. Get a pan that is 9 by 13 and grease it with cooking spray.
2. Place everything in the pan except the chicken and seasoning in the pan.
3. Place the chicken on top of the rest of the ingredients and place seasoning on top of the chicken.
4. Bake at 375 for 45 minutes.
5. Place the cheese on the top and bake for 5 minutes more.
6. Top with green onions.

This recipe will give you four servings.
This recipe will take you an hour to complete.

Chicken & Rice Casserole

The ingredients for this recipe are as follows:

- ★   4 breasts of chicken
- ★   A cup and a half of water
- ★   A single of white rice that is uncooked and long grain
- ★   A single package of onion soup mix
- ★   A single 10 ounce can of cream of mushroom soup that is condensed

The steps to complete this recipe are as follows:

1. Heat your oven to 325 F.
2. Get a 9 by 13 pan and spray it with cooking spray.
3. Add your chicken and season it (with pepper and salt)
4. Pour the rice over the chicken. The rice should be uncooked.
5. Sprinkle with the soup mix.
6. Combine the water and the soup and pour it over the chicken.
7. Cover it and then bake it for an hour and fifteen minutes. The rice should be tender.

This recipe will give you 4 servings.

This recipe will take you an hour and a half to complete.

Nutritional information (per serving):

- ➢   Calories-470
- ➢   Fat- 7 grams
- ➢   Carbs- 40 grams
- ➢   Protein- 54 grams

Chapter 8: Baked Snack Recipes

Cheddar Biscuits

The ingredients for this recipe are as follows:

★   2 cups of biscuit mix

★   A quarter cup of butter

★   ⅔ of a cup of milk

★   A single cup of mild cheddar cheese that is shredded

★   A quarter teaspoon of garlic powder

The steps to complete this recipe are as follows:

1.   Heat your oven to 450 F.

2.   Grease a baking sheet.

3.   Mix the biscuit mix, milk, and cheese in a bowl. Make sure that the batter is doughy and soft. A wooden spoon will help with this, and it should take half a minute.

4.   Put the batter on the sheet in spoonfuls.

5.   Bake 10 minutes, and the biscuits should be a light brown.

6.   Heat the garlic and butter in a pan on low heat until it is melted. This will take 5 minutes.

7.   Brush that mix over the biscuits.

This recipe will take 20 minutes to complete.

Nutritional information (per serving):

➢   Calories-385

➢   Fat-24.6 grams

➢   Carbs-31.5 grams

➢   Protein-10.2 grams

Almond-Raisin Granola

The ingredients for this recipe are as follows:

- ★ Half a cup of flax seeds
- ★ Half a cup of sunflower seed kernels
- ★ A cup of raw almonds that are sliced
- ★ 3 cups of oats that are old-fashioned
- ★ A quarter cup of melted coconut oil
- ★ A single cup of raisins
- ★ 6 tablespoons of honey
- ★ 6 tablespoons of pure maple syrup
- ★ 2 tablespoons of water that is warm

The steps to complete this recipe are as follows:

1. Heat your oven to 250 and line a jelly roll pan with baking parchment.
2. Mix everything but the water, oil, honey, and syrup in a bowl and whisk the water, oil, honey, and syrup in another bowl. Make sure that the honey mix is smooth.
3. Pour the oat mix bowl into the honey bowl.
4. Spread the mix on the pan in a layer that is even.
5. Bake for an hour but up to an hour and a half until the color is a golden brown.
6. Take out of the oven and make sure that you let it cool completely.
7. Take the granola off by lifting the paper.
8. Break it and place in a bowl adding your choice of ingredients and then mix it.
9. Store in a container that is airtight.

This recipe will take you an hour and 45 minutes to complete.

Nutritional information (per serving):

- ➢ Calories-568
- ➢ Protein-12.4 grams
- ➢ Fat-27.2 grams
- ➢ Carbs0-76.4 grams

Banana Bread

The ingredients for this recipe are as follows:

- ★ A single teaspoon of baking soda
- ★ ¾ of a cup of sugar
- ★ Half a cup of pecans that have been chopped
- ★ 3 bananas medium in size and mashed
- ★ Half a cup of mayonnaise
- ★ A single egg
- ★ A cup and a half of flour

The steps to complete this recipe are as follows:

1. Preheat your oven to 350.
2. Get a bowl.
3. Mix together the egg, mayo, and bananas.
4. Get another bowl.
5. Mix the baking soda, pecans, flour, and sugar in the bowl.
6. Add the flour mix to the wet mix and stir until combined.
7. The mix will be very thick; this is alright. If you over-mix, it won't be right.
8. Grease a pan.
9. Pour the mix into the pan and bake for an hour. A toothpick should come out clean.
10. Remove from the pan and make sure it cools completely.

This recipe will give you a dozen servings.

You will need an hour and ten minutes to complete this recipe.

Nutritional information (per serving):

- ➢ Calories-231

- ➢ Fat-10 grams
- ➢ Fiber- 1 gram
- ➢ Protein-2 grams
- ➢ Carbs-31 grams

Croissants

The ingredients for this recipe are as follows:

- ★ A single cup of milk
- ★ 4 cups of flour that is all-purpose
- ★ A third of a cup of sugar that is granulated
- ★ 2 and a quarter teaspoons of salt that is kosher
- ★ 4 teaspoons of yeast that is active and dry
- ★ A cup and a quarter of butter that is cold and unsalted
- ★ An egg wash (this is to have a single large egg, and you beat it with a teaspoon of water)

The steps to complete this recipe are as follows:

1. Place your yeast and salt along with the flour and sugar in a bowl and whisk it all together until it has combined well.

2. Slice your butter into slices an eighth of an inch thick and toss it into the flour mix so that the butter is coated.

3. Add your milk in and stir it together. A stiff dough will be made.

4. Wrap your dough and make sure it's tight. You are going to use plastic wrap. Let it chill for 60 minutes.

5. Get yourself a lightly floured surface and roll your dough into a big rectangle that is long.

6. Fold and make it like a letter. This means you fold it into thirds. Turn it 90 degrees and repeat 4 times.

7. The dough should be flat and smooth with streaks of butter in it.

8. Rewrap it again and chill for another 60 minutes. Divide the dough in half and then roll again.

9. It should be an eighth of an inch thick.

10. Cut your dough into triangles that are long and skinny.

11. Notch your wide end of each triangle you made with a half-inch cut.

12. Roll from the wide end to the end with a point. Tuck the point under the croissant.

13. Place on a baking sheet that is lined with parchment.

14. Cover with plastic wrap (loosely) and allow it to proof for 120 minutes.

15. Preheat your oven to 375 F.

16. Brush the croissants with your egg wash.

17. Bake 20 minutes.

18. They should be puffy brown golden color, and they should be flaky.

This recipe will give you a dozen croissants.

This recipe will take you an hour to finish.

Nutritional information (per serving):

➢   Calories-294

➢   Fat-16 grams

➢   Protein- 5 grams

➢   Fiber- 1 gram

➢   Carbs-31 grams

Jam Pockets

The ingredients for this recipe are as follows:

- ★ A single teaspoon of vanilla
- ★ A single egg
- ★ 2 cups of flour
- ★ Half a cup of powdered sugar
- ★ A single cup of butter that is cut into cubes and cold

The steps to complete this recipe are as follows:

1. Preheat your oven to 375.
2. Use a food processor and combine your sugar and flour until they have mixed.
3. Toss in your butter and give it a few long buzzes with it until it has a cornmeal look.
4. Add the vanilla and egg and then buzz it twice more. You should be left with a soft dough.
5. Cover with plastic wrap and then let it chill in the fridge for a couple of hours.
6. Roll out our dough and use a cookie cutter to make circles.
7. Add the jam of your choice to the center and fold your edges inward. It should overlap in the middle.
8. Bake 10 minutes.
9. The bottom should be a faint brown color.
10. When cooled, sprinkle sugar over the top.

This recipe will give you 2 dozen pockets.
This recipe will take you 2 hours and 20 minutes to finish.

Pizza Pockets

The ingredients for this recipe are as follows:

- ★ A third of a cup of Parmesan that is grated
- ★ A quarter of a cup of Parmesan that is grated
- ★ 8 ounces of turkey sausage (Italian)
- ★ A single tablespoon of olive oil
- ★ A single egg beaten
- ★ A single cup and a half of marinara sauce
- ★ All-purpose flour
- ★ A single pizza crust store-bought
- ★ 4 ounces of room temperature cream cheese
- ★ A cup of arugula tightly packed

The steps to complete this recipe are as follows:

1. Heat your olive oil over a heat that is medium-high and in a medium heavy skillet.
2. Add in the sausage and cook until it is golden and crumbled. 5 minutes.
3. Add the arugula and cook it until it has wilted.
4. Turn off your heat and let it cool for 19 minutes.
5. Add in your cream cheese and a third of the parmesan.
6. Stir, so it combines.
7. Set it aside.
8. Preheat your oven to 400 F.
9. Roll out your dough and make a big rectangle.
10. Cut it in half.
11. Do this again until you have eight equal rectangles.
12. Put your toppings onto one of the sides of each rectangle.
13. Brush the edges with egg wash.
14. Close the rectangle of dough over the topping.

15. Use a fork to seal them up.

16. Put the pockets on the baking sheet that is lined with parchment paper.

17. Brush the tops with egg wash.

18. Sprinkle the rest of the cheese on top.

19. Bake for 15 minutes.

20. Heat your marinara sauce over a heat that is low.

21. Serve with sauce when done.

This recipe will give you 4 servings

This recipe will take you 40 minutes to finish

Nutritional information (per serving):

➢ Calories-385

➢ Fat- 19 grams

➢ Carbs-37 grams

➢ Protein-17 grams

➢ Fiber-1.5 grams

Smoky Pretzel Mix

The ingredients for this recipe are as follows:

- ★   A single cup of almonds that are smoked
- ★   A single cup of mini pretzels
- ★   2 teaspoons of chipotle chili powder
- ★   A single teaspoon of paprika that is smoked
- ★   2 cups corn snack crackers
- ★   2 cups rice cereal squares
- ★   2 cups of white cheddar cheese crackers in bite-size
- ★   6 tablespoons of butter that is unsalted

The steps you need to complete are as follows:

1. Heat the oven to 325.
2. Toss everything together except the butter and spices in a bowl.
3. Melt the butter in a pan over medium heat.
4. Stir in chili powder, paprika and garlic.
5. Drizzle over the mix.
6. Toss to coat evenly.
7. Spread it on a rimmed baking sheet that you lined with parchment paper.
8. Bake for 12 minutes. Stir once during this time.
9. Cool totally on the sheet.
10. Store in a container that is airtight.

This recipe will give you 10 servings.

This recipe will take a half-hour to complete.

Blueberry Pound Cake

The ingredients for this recipe are as follows:

- ★ 2 Tablespoons of butter
- ★ A quarter cup of white sugar
- ★ 2 ¾ cups of all-purpose flour
- ★ A single teaspoon of baking powder
- ★ A single cup of butter
- ★ 4 eggs
- ★ 2 cups of white sugar
- ★ 2 cups of blueberries that are fresh
- ★ A single teaspoon of vanilla extract
- ★ A quarter cup of flour that is all-purpose

The steps to complete this recipe are as follows:

1. Preheat your oven to 325 F.
2. grease a pan that is 10 inches with 2 tablespoons of butter.
3. Sprinkle that same pan with a quarter cup of sugar.
4. Mix 2 ¾ of the cup of flour with the baking powder and place to the side.
5. Get a bowl and cream a cup of butter and 2 cups of sugar together until it has become fluffy and light.
6. Beat the eggs one at a time before stirring the vanilla in.
7. Slowly beat in your flour mix.
8. Dredge your berries with the last quarter cup of flour.
9. Fold into the batter before pouring it in your prepared pan.
10. Bake for 80 minutes. The toothpick test should show a clean toothpick.
11. Let cool for 10 minutes into the pan before letting it totally cool on a wire rack.

This recipe will take you 90 minutes to finish

Nutritional information (per serving):

- ➢ Calories-338
- ➢ Fat-14.5 grams
- ➢ Carbs-48.8 grams
- ➢ Protein-4.3 grams

Zucchini Bread

This recipe will need the following ingredients:

- ★ Half a teaspoon of baking powder
- ★ Half a teaspoon of all-purpose flour
- ★ Half a teaspoon of baking soda
- ★ Half a teaspoon of ground cinnamon
- ★ Half a cup of unsweetened applesauce
- ★ A single cup and a half of zucchini that has been lightly packed but not drained of liquid and grated
- ★ A single cup of granulated sugar
- ★ A quarter cup of packed brown sugar (light)
- ★ 2 eggs (large)
- ★ A single teaspoon of vanilla extract
- ★ A third of a cup of vegetable oil

You will need to complete the following steps:

1. Heat your oven to 350 F.
2. Get a 9 by 5 loaf pan and spray it with cooking spray.
3. Get a bowl and add everything in but the baking powder , flour, and cinnamon along with the baking soda.
4. Whisk all of these together until they have combined well.
5. Add in the cinnamon and baking soda along with the flour and baking powder and stir until there is no dry flour remains. Do not over mix this, however.
6. Pour the batter in the pan and bake for 50 minutes. A toothpick should have moist crumbs on it.
7. Cool for 10 minutes.
8. Move to a cooling rack and let it cool totally.

This recipe will give you a dozen servings.

You will need an hour and 10 minutes to complete this recipe.

Nutritional information (per serving):

- ➢ Calories-213
- ➢ Carbs-35 grams
- ➢ Protein-3 grams
- ➢ Fat- 7 grams

Lemon Raspberry Muffins

This recipe will require the following ingredients:

- ★ Half a cup of honey
- ★ 2 eggs
- ★ A single cup of plain Greek yogurt
- ★ A single cup and ¾ of white whole wheat flour
- ★ A single teaspoon of baking powder
- ★ Half a teaspoon of baking soda
- ★ A third of a cup of coconut oil that is melted
- ★ 2 teaspoons of vanilla extract
- ★ The zest from a lemon
- ★ A single cup and a half of organic raspberries
- ★ A single tablespoon of turbinado sugar

The steps that you will need to take to complete this recipe is the following:

1. Heat your oven to 350 F.
2. Grease a 12 cup muffin tin with coconut oil or cooking spray.
3. Get a large bowl.
4. Combine flour, baking soda, baking powder, and blend together with a whisk.
5. Get another bowl and combine the honey oil, and beat them together with a whisk.
6. Add in the eggs and beat them well before adding the zest, vanilla, and yogurt.
7. Mix it all well. If the oil gets solid, microwave it for half a minute.
8. Pour your wet ingredients into the dry.
9. Mix it with a large spoon until it has just combined.
10. Fold raspberries in the batter. It will be thick.
11. Divided into the 12 cups and add sugar to the top.
12. Bake 24 minutes and toothpick should come out clean.
13. Let cool on a cooling rack.

This recipe will give you 12 2 servings.

This recipe will take you an hour to finish.

Nutritional information (per serving):

- ➢ Calories-193
- ➢ Fat-7.5 grams
- ➢ Carbs-28.7 grams
- ➢ Protein-5.3 grams

CHAPTER 9: BAKED DESSERT RECIPES

Chocolate Cake

This recipe will require the following ingredients:

- ★ 2 cups of white sugar
- ★ A cup and a 3/4 of flour that is all-purpose
- ★ 2 eggs
- ★ A single cup of milk
- ★ Half a cup of vegetable oil
- ★ ¾ of a cup of cocoa powder that has been unsweetened
- ★ A single teaspoon and a half of baking powder
- ★ A single teaspoon and a half of baking soda
- ★ 2 teaspoons of vanilla extract
- ★ A single cup of water that is boiling

The steps that you will need to take to complete this recipe is the following:

1. Heat the oven to 350 F.
2. Grease and flour 2 round pans that are 9 inches.
3. Get a bowl.
4. Mix everything in a bowl but the eggs, vanilla, and oil. Don't use the water ye either.
5. Stir everything together.
6. Add the oil, vanilla, and eggs, and the milk and mix for 2 minutes with a mixe on medium speed.
7. Stir in the water.
8. Pour in the pans.
9. Bake for a half-hour.
10. Cool for 10 minutes before you move to a wire rack.

This recipe will take you an hour to finish.

Nutritional information (per serving):

➢ Calories-157

➢ Fat-5.7 grams

➢ Carbs-25.7 grams

➢ Protein-2.3 grams

Carrot Cake

The ingredients you will need is the following:

- ★   2 teaspoons of cinnamon that is ground
- ★   2 cups of flour that is all-purpose
- ★   2 cups of white sugar
- ★   4 eggs
- ★   A single cup and a quarter of vegetable oil
- ★   2 teaspoons of extract of vanilla
- ★   2 teaspoons of baking soda
- ★   2 teaspoons of baking powder
- ★   3 cups of carrots that are grated
- ★   A single cup of pecans that are chopped
- ★   Half a cup of softened butter
- ★   A teaspoon of extract of vanilla
- ★   4 cups of confectioner's sugar
- ★   8 ounces of softened cream cheese
- ★   A single cup of pecans that are chopped

The steps you will need to take to complete this dish are as follows:

1.   Heat your oven to 350.
2.   Get a bowl and set it aside before you get a pan that is 9 by 13 and you grease and flour it.
3.   Beat your eggs, vanilla, sugar, and oil together.
4.   Mix in the baking powder and soda along with your cinnamon and flour.
5.   Then stir in the carrots before you fold in your pecans.
6.   Pour the mix in the pan that you prepared for the oven.
7.   Bake for 50 minutes and then let cool for ten before you move it to a wire rack.
8.   Let cool totally.

For the topping:

1.   Get a bowl and combine everything before beating it. When it's creamy, add in the pecans that are chopped.

2.   Put it on top.

This will take you two hours to complete.

Nutritional information (per serving):

➢   Calories-575

➢   Fat-34.8

➢   Carbs-63.7 grams

Cheesecake

This recipe will require the following ingredients:

- ★ A single cup of sour cream
- ★ 2 Teaspoons of vanilla
- ★ 3 eggs
- ★ 3 (8 ounce) packages of softened cream cheese
- ★ A third of a cup of divided sugar
- ★ A third of a cup of melted butter
- ★ A cup and ¾ of graham cracker crumbs
- ★ A single can of cherry pie filling (go for 21 ounces)

The steps that you will need to take to complete this recipe is the following:

1. Heat your oven to 350.
2. Mix the crumbs, sugar and butter and press into a springform pan that is 9 inches.
3. Beat the cream cheese and leftover sugar using a mixer.
4. Mix until it is blended.
5. Add vanilla and sour cream, and make sure to mix it all well before adding in your egg. Go one at a time and beat it all on low speed.
6. Pour it over the crust.
7. Bake for 60 minutes.
8. You can top it with the filling.

Nutritional information (per serving):

- ➤ Calories-313
- ➤ Fat-17.7 grams
- ➤ Carbs-35.8 grams

Brownies

This recipe will require the following ingredients:

- ★ A third of a cup of cocoa powder that is unsweetened
- ★ Half a cup of all-purpose flour
- ★ 2 eggs
- ★ A single cup of white sugar
- ★ Half a cup of butter
- ★ A single teaspoon of vanilla extract
- ★ A quarter of a teaspoon of baking powder

The icing

- ★ A single tablespoon of honey
- ★ A single teaspoon of vanilla extract
- ★ A single cup of confectioners sugar
- ★ 3 tablespoons of softened butter
- ★ 3 tablespoon of cocoa powder that is unsweetened

The steps that you will need to take to complete this recipe is the following:

1. Preheat your oven to 350.
2. Get a pan and melt the butter.
3. Take it away from the heat and add in the sugar, egg, and vanilla.
4. Stir it and then beat in the flour, cocoa and baking powder.
5. Spread in a pan that is prepared.
6. Bake a half hour.

For the icing:

1. Combine everything and stir it.
2. Put it on the brownie.

This recipe will take you an hour to finish.

Nutritional information (per serving):

- ➢ Calories-183
- ➢ Fat-9 grams
- ➢ Carbs-25.7 grams

Blondies

This recipe will require the following ingredients:

- ★ A single cup of melted and unsalted butter
- ★ 2 and a half cups of flour that is all-purpose
- ★ 2 large eggs and a single egg yolk
- ★ A cup and a quarter of brown sugar that has been tightly packed
- ★ Half a cup of sugar
- ★ 2 teaspoons of vanilla extract
- ★ A single cup of walnuts that are chopped
- ★ ⅔ of a cup of white chocolate chips
- ★ Half of a teaspoon of baking powder
- ★ 2 teaspoons of cornstarch

The steps that you will need to take to complete this recipe is the following:

1. Preheat your oven to 350 F.
2. Line a 13 by 9 pan with parchment paper.
3. Combine your sugar and melted butter in a bowl.
4. Add your yolk, eggs, and vanilla extract and then stir until everything has been fully combined.
5. Set this to the side.
6. In another bowl, whisk your other ingredients together except the nuts and chocolate chips.
7. Then fold the nuts and chips in.
8. Put the batter in the pan.
9. Put it in the oven and bake for a half-hour.
10. Let cool.

This recipe will give you 15 servings.

This recipe will take you an hour to finish.

Nutritional information (per serving):

- ➢ Calories-370
- ➢ Fat-20 grams
- ➢ Carbs-46 grams
- ➢ Protein-4 grams

Chocolate Chip Cookies

This recipe will require the following ingredients:

★ A single cup of softened butter

★ 2 eggs

★ 2 teaspoons of vanilla extract

★ A single teaspoon of baking soda

★ A single cup of white sugar

★ A single cup of brown sugar that is packed

★ 2 cups of chocolate chips that are semi-sweet

★ 3 cups of all-purpose flour

★ A single cup of walnuts that are chopped

★ 2 teaspoons of hot water

The steps that you will need to take to complete this recipe is the following:

1. Heat the oven to 350 F.
2. Cream together the sugar and butter until it's smooth.
3. Beat in your eggs one at a time and stir in your vanilla.
4. Dissolve the baking soda in your hot water.
5. Add in the butter before stirring in the nuts and chips.
6. Drop spoonfuls onto a pan.
7. Bake 1o minutes.

This recipe will take you an hour to finish

Nutritional information (per serving):

➢ Calories-298

➢ Fat-15.6 grams

➢ Carbs-38.8 grams

➢ Protein-3.6 grams

Snickerdoodles

This recipe will require the following ingredients:

- ★ 2 eggs
- ★ Half of a cup of shortening
- ★ A half of a cup of softened butter
- ★ A cup and a half of white sugar
- ★ 2 teaspoons of cinnamon that is ground
- ★ 2 tablespoons of white sugar
- ★ 2 teaspoons of extract of vanilla
- ★ A single teaspoon of baking soda
- ★ 2 teaspoons of tartar (cream of tartar)
- ★ 2 ¾ cups of flour that is all-purpose

The steps that you will need to take to complete this recipe is the following:

1. Heat up your 400 F.
2. Cream the butter, sugar, eggs, vanilla, and shortening before blending in tartar soda and flour.
3. Shape your dough and put it into balls.
4. Mix up your sugar (the tablespoons) and cinnamon.
5. Roll your dough in that mix.
6. Bake 10 minutes.
7. Remove right away from the baking sheets.

This recipe will take you an hour to finish

Nutritional information (per serving):

- ➢ Calories-92
- ➢ Fat-4.3 grams
- ➢ Carbs-12.4 grams

Apple Pie

This recipe will require the following ingredients:

- ★ A quarter teaspoon of ground ginger
- ★ Half a cup of sugar
- ★ Half a cup of brown sugar that is packed
- ★ A single teaspoon of cinnamon that is ground
- ★ 3 tablespoons of flour that is all-purpose
- ★ A single tablespoon of lemon juice from a lemon
- ★ A single tablespoon of butter
- ★ A single, double-crust pie
- ★ Half a dozen tart apples that are sliced thinly
- ★ A single white large egg
- ★ A quarter teaspoon of nutmeg that is ground

The steps that you will need to take to complete this recipe is the following:

1. Get a bowl and combine the spices, flour, and sugars.
2. In another bowl, put in the lemon juice and toss the apples in it.
3. Add in the sugar mix and toss so they are coated.
4. Line the pie plate with bottom crust and trim so that it is even with the edge.
5. Fill it with the apple mix and dot with butter.
6. Roll the rest of the crust on top to fit the top.
7. Place it over the filling.
8. Trim before sealing and fluting the edges.
9. Cut slits into the crust.
10. Beat the egg white until it becomes foamy and brush it over that crust.
11. Place sugar over it.
12. Cover those edges with foil but do it loosely.
13. Bake for 25 minutes at a heat of 375.

14.   Take off the foil and bake until the crust is a golden brown color and the filling is nice and bubbly.

15.   This will take an additional 25 minutes.

16.   Let it cool on a wire rack.

This recipe will give you eight servings.

This recipe will take you an hour and 20 minutes to finish.

Nutritional information (per serving):

➢   Calories-414

➢   Fat-16 grams

➢   Carbs-67 grams

Coffee Cake

This recipe will require the following ingredients:

For your topping:

★ A single cup of flour that is all-purpose

★ A single tablespoon and a half of cinnamon that is ground

★ A single cup of brown sugar that is light

★ Half a dozen tablespoons of melted butter

For the cake itself:

★ A single cup of sugar that is granulated

★ A single cup of room temperature butter

★ 3/4 of a cup of sour cream

★ 3 teaspoons of baking powder

★ ⅔ of a cup of brown sugar that is light

★ 3 eggs

★ A single tablespoon of vanilla extract

★ A single cup and a quarter of milk

★ 3 ⅔ cup of flour that is all-purpose

For the filling:

★ ¾ of a cup of flour that is all-purpose

★ 2 teaspoons of cinnamon that is ground

★ ¾ of a cup of brown sugar that is light

For the icing:

★ 2-3 tablespoons of milk

★ A single cup of powdered sugar

The steps that you will need to take to complete this recipe is the following:

1.   Make sure that your oven is heated to 350 F.
2.   Get a 9 by 13 baking dish and spray with nonstick spray.
3.   Place to the side.
4.   Get a bowl and whisk together the items for the filling before putting it to the side as well.
5.   For the topping mix everything together in a bowl, and it should look like crumbs. Form pieces with your hands. Place to the side.
6.   As for the cake, mix your sugar and butter in a bowl and use a mixer at medium speed for 120 seconds.
7.   It should be fluffy and light.
8.   You need to add in the sour cream, vanilla, eggs, and baking powder and mix for 60 seconds. It should be combined, and it should be smooth as well.
9.   Put your mixer to a low setting and add in the milk and flour (alternating the portions) begin with the flour, end with the flour.
10. Mix until it is smooth and just combined.
11. Spread half of the batter in the pan and sprinkle the filling over the top. Then place the remaining batter on top.
12. Place the topping on top.
13. Bake for 45 minutes.
14. Remove from the oven and place on a wire rack.
15. Let it totally cool.
16. Drizzle the icing on top.

This recipe will give you a dozen servings

This recipe will take you an hour and 5 minutes to finish

Nutritional information (per serving):

➢   Calories-660
➢   Fat-24.9 grams

- ➢ Carbs-101.1 grams
- ➢ Protein-9.6 grams

Lemon Bars

This recipe will require the following ingredients:

- ★ A single cup of softened butter
- ★ A single cup and a half of white sugar
- ★ A quarter cup of all-purpose flour
- ★ Half a cup of white sugar
- ★ 2 juiced lemons

The steps that you will need to take to complete this recipe is the following:

1. Heat your oven to 350 F.
2. Get a bowl.
3. Blend half a cup of sugar and 2 cups of flour along with butter that has softened.
4. Get a 9 by 13 pan and press it into the bottom.
5. Bake 20 minutes.
6. Get a bowl.
7. Whisk a quarter cup of flour and a cup and a half of a cup of sugar.
8. Whisk in the lemon juice and the eggs.
9. Pour over the crust.
10. Bake another 20 minutes.
11. They will firm as they cool.

This recipe will take you an hour to finish

Nutritional information (per serving):

- ➢ Calories-126
- ➢ Fat-5.8 grams
- ➢ Carbs-17.8 grams
- ➢ Protein-1.6 grams

CHAPTER 10: IDEAS FOR MORE BAKING FUN

Baking is a really fun thing to do not just as yourself while you're trying to grow your skills and learn how to cook and bake properly to become the best chef that you can be, it's also a really great way to open up your creativity and have fun with your family. Baking has long since been a family tradition, and it's a great way to learn some quality time in the kitchen as well. It brings families together and friends together and can create a great sense of community. All it takes is a couple of recipes, some ingredients and to know what it is that you want to make or an idea that you want to try.

It's also a lot more satisfying than being stuck on social media for five hours. This is a trap that many fall into. You already know what celebrities are doing and what fashion is trending right now. As such, you don't need to spend half a day on Instagram. Instead, why not makes an irresistible dish in the kitchen and your skills to become better and make better food? Some great things that you can make and some great ideas for more baking fun are to try making some of the following items for yourself.

- ❖ Banana scones-you can make them vegan or gluten-free, depending on what you put in them.
- ❖ A giant brownie
- ❖ You can make pull-apart cinnamon rolls as well. The reason that we mentioned these though we've already had a recipe above is because there are literally hundreds of different ways to do a cinnamon roll and each one is unique to the baker.
- ❖ Donuts. You don't have to go traditional here. You can make donuts which are different than other donuts that you see every day. Instead of making chocolate or vanilla or something that's everywhere else that you go, you could try making a cream cheese donut or an herb encrusted donut instead.
- ❖ Chocolate chip cupcakes with avocado icing or strawberry icing instead of the typical vanilla icing.

You can honestly make just about anything as long as you're creative. Everyone is also looking for great ways to be healthy, so instead of just making sweet and decadent desserts, you could also try these ideas for people who are more healthy options. If you are one of those or wish to cook for them, try these.

❖ Baked fruit-there are many different ways that you can do this, and there are literally thousands of ingredients that you can use for these recipes.

❖ You can make baked apples with nuts, or you can bake peaches as well.

❖ In addition to this, you can make grapefruit and pineapple, mangos and many other fruits that would taste amazing in a baked dish.

❖ Another example of this is scones. Scones are a great British dish, and you can make them with dark chocolate or oranges, you can make them with strawberries blueberries, there are a lot of healthy ingredients that you can use that would make this a great dessert.

❖ Another great idea is to do something like a cheesecake that has hundreds of different variations as well.

Following unique trends can be fun as well, and a great example here would be the Funfetti cupcakes. These are cupcakes that are Instagram worthy and are covered with different sprinkles and flavors. You could also turn the salty dish into a sweet dish by making chocolate chip stuffed pretzels or making chocolate covered pretzels. Turning salty into sweet can be really fun and turning salty or sweet and savory can take some real creativity and talent.

For a new popular idea, you could try to begin making banana bread, but you could also put a twist on this as well. Instead of just making regular banana bread, you can make blueberry banana bread, strawberry banana bread, raisin bread or get really innovative and try something like papaya bread or mango bread for a new twist. If you like tiramisu, you could make something new and different like tiramisu cupcakes instead of just regular cupcakes or regular tiramisu. This adds a twist that lets them see how creative you really are. When you're baking the options are endless, it just depends on your own creativity

You can use your imagination to take you to the limit or find that your mind and passion have no limit. Another example is that if it's fall, you can make cookies in the shapes of leaves. By that same token, if it's winter, you can make snowflakes. On somebody's birthday, you could bake a cake in numbers or letters and you can have baking ideas that are based on your favorite movies if you like such as Disney or Paw Patrol for a child's birthday party. You can make cupcakes or cookies look like the characters from their favorite movies and this would bring a massive delight to the people around you. Another good example is if it's Halloween, you could bake monster cookies with little eyes or Dracula cookies with little fangs.

Take holidays and ideas from other cultures as well. If it's Cinco de Mayo or another holiday that is cultural, you can learn about their culture and see what would be appropriate and fun to make. If you find that you are getting bored following trends is also another great way to keep your creativity flowing. For example, unicorn cake is a very popular dish as well right now, and it's because everybody has uncovered their obsession with unicorns and Instagram. Everyone wants to take beautiful pictures and show everybody what they can do and this is something that you can do too and make your own wonderful creations. This wouldn't be the main goal here of course, but it is a great example of showing how social media does play a part in what you can make because it will give you fresh ideas. The trick here is not to get stuck on it so that you're so focused on it instead of other things like that ideas and the dishes that you want to make for yourself.

CHAPTER 11: BAKING IDEAS TO DO TOGETHER

In this chapter, we will be giving you a few ideas on baking that you can do together. I you want to bake as a family, a great thing that you can learn how to do is desserts. You can also help with other meals as well. Breakfast, lunch, dinner, and snacks are all things that you can help them with too or they can help you. These are all important parts of the day and they all give you different nutritional value as well as playing a different structura part in your day. As a chef, you need to know which meal is going to give you the mos benefit and what is going to make the people around you happy. When you are a che you're not just cooking for yourself but you're cooking for the people around you and you want them to have a wonderful experience with your food. You want them to be able to fee what you're feeling with your dishes and you want them to be able to feel your passion and creativity. When your baking, it can be a lovely experience that makes you happy and fee great about yourself.

There are many different ways that you can have fun and bake together, and the firs thing that you need to do in order to achieve this is you could all go shopping together fo the ingredients. That is where the baking starts and you can not bake without the prope tools. You could work on the recipe together and begin to start the process together as well. Just being together in the kitchen will give you a sense of camaraderie as a family and it will bring you closer together with the people you care about. Cooking and baking is a great way to bond and you hear many stories from grandparents and mothers about hov they used to bake cakes and pies around the holidays with their families or their loved ones. This is something that you can do too and it's a great way to have more fun baking together.

There's also a lot of different recipes that you can try when you're just starting out. Man people start out with deserts because they have a sweet tooth or vanilla-like food that i considered to be junk food but in keeping our bodies as healthy as possible, there's also a lot of new ingredients that you can use as well that are found in health food such as fruits and vegetables. You can bake with all of these ingredients as well which is a great idea for when you're trying to learn how to do this together and have fun. One of the great things about this if you want to do this as a family is to assign jobs to everybody. Have one person read through the ingredients, have the other person read the recipe as well. You could have one person be the cleaning person, one person watching the oven and helping with making sure that everything is going all right, but the best part is you can all taste the dish as you're making it. This is a great way to work as a team and bake together.

You can work on the recipes together and make sure that the food is being prepared in the proper way, and then at the end of the day, you have something that you've created together and it's something that's beautiful. This is ultimately what brings the family together. Making memories together and having fun making these dishes. It is what makes people want to bake. Some great ideas for baking together and recipes that would be easy to try while you're still learning are the following:

- ❖ Fruity cream cake
- ❖ Chocolate chip cookie bars
- ❖ Peach cake with a mango drizzle
- ❖ monkey bread (which is a popular southern staple)
- ❖ biscuits
- ❖ cobbler
- ❖ coffee cake
- ❖ individual mixed berry cake
- ❖ crumb bars
- ❖ granola bars
- ❖ cookies such as Funfetti or peanut butter
- ❖ pie
- ❖ brownies

You could try casseroles like macaroni and other pasta dishes as well. Many pasta dishes are actually baked in the oven, which surprises people but it's not always about making things on a stove. Casseroles are a big thing in today's society and there are literally thousands of different variations of casseroles that you can make. You can also bake meats and other dishes like the following.

- ❖ Green bean casserole
- ❖ Sweet potatoes
- ❖ chicken
- ❖ Turkey
- ❖ Ham

It's literally an endless opportunity to be together as a family, which will create a more fun environment that you want to keep baking in.

Chapter 12: Basic Nutrition and Why It's Important

So what do we mean by "basic nutrition" or "good nutrition?" We mean getting all the nutrients, goods, ingredients, and things that are necessary for proper growth, health, and balance. It's important to eat all the right things, and when we do eat some of the less healthy things, that we're still keeping our intake balanced. Keeping a proper balance of the foods that we eat can help us to sleep, think, breathe, and function in the way that we're supposed to and it can keep us feeling our very best!

Remember the Nutritional Facts labels we talked about at the beginning of the book? Those are the labels that tell us what we're eating and how those foods would help us in our efforts to eat healthy and to keep our diets balanced. Those little percentages on the label tell us how much of those things we should be having each day so our diets are nice and balanced! As mentioned when we talked about those Nutritional Facts labels, you can get pretty sick if you spend a long time in your life eating too many of the wrong foods and not enough of the right foods. That's why doctors and scientists have come together to make helpful guidelines that we can follow to eat all the right things and to keep the not-so-good things in a healthy balance. When you're trying to put together a meal, you want to make sure that your meals are put together, so the amounts of the foods on your plate look a lot like this one here:

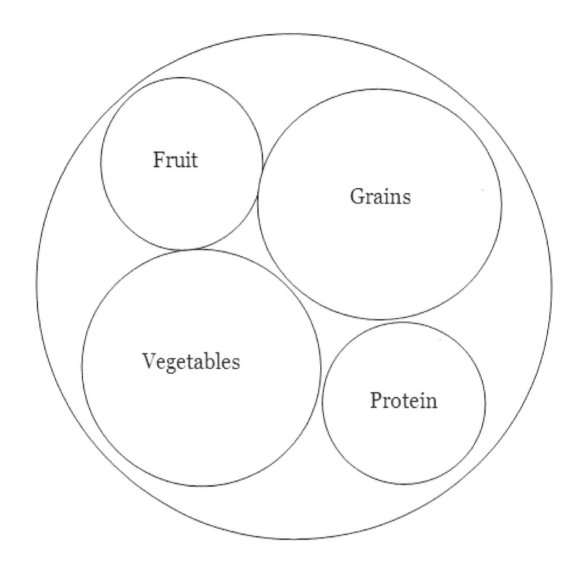

Each day, you want to make sure that you're getting enough protein, healthy fats, natural sugar, and complex carbohydrates that your body can break down and use for energy all day long. A breakfast of eggs, toast, and yogurt is a great way to start your day with protein, carbs, and healthy fats. A breakfast of chocolate sugary cereal and a donut might leave you bouncing off the walls for a couple of hours and then cranky and sleepy until lunch, so it's best to avoid those kinds of things! This is the food pyramid. This chart shows the types of foods you should be eating the most of in the larger parts of the pyramid. You want a strong, large base filled with healthy fruits and vegetables, and then you want to have less and less of each of the items as you work your way up the pyramid.

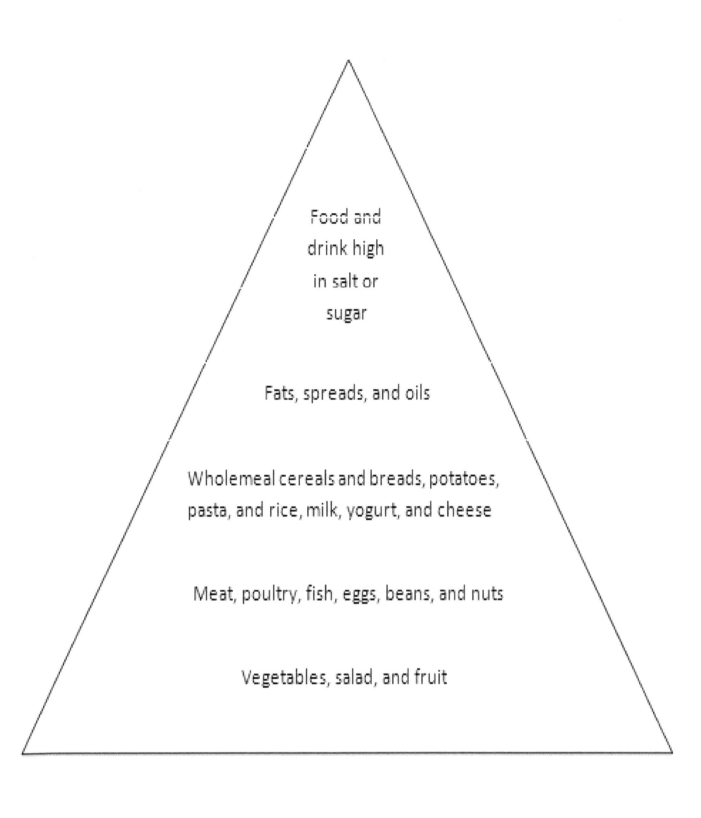

Food and drink high in salt or sugar

Fats, spreads, and oils

Wholemeal cereals and breads, potatoes, pasta, and rice, milk, yogurt, and cheese

Meat, poultry, fish, eggs, beans, and nuts

Vegetables, salad, and fruit

Conclusion

Thank you for making it through to the end of **Kid Chef: Young Chef Cookbook - The Complete Baking Book for Kids Who Love to Bake and Eat**, let's hope it was informative and able to provide you with all of the tools you need to achieve your goals whatever they may be.

The next step is to try each of the recipes in this book and test your baking skills. You will want to make sure that you try lots of new things in the kitchen to discover new flavors, new recipes, new foods, and to push the boundaries of what you know.

Baking is such a great passion for having and there are so many resources out there for you to use. Always look out for new skills that you can learn to make your time in the kitchen more fun and more rewarding.